NOBODY HATES TRUMP MORE THAN TRUMP:

AN INTERVENTION

DAVID SHIELDS

THOUGHT
CATALOG
Books

This book was designed by KJ Parish and published by Thought Catalog Books, a publishing house owned by The Thought & Expression Company.

10 9 8 7 6 5 4 3 2 1

ISBN 978-1-949759-05-1

For Melanie Thernstrom

ALSO BY DAVID SHIELDS

The Trouble with Men: Reflections on Sex, Love, Marriage, Porn, and Power (forthcoming)

Other People: Takes & Mistakes

War Is Beautiful: The New York Times *Pictorial Guide to the Glamour of Armed Conflict*

That Thing You Do with Your Mouth: The Sexual Autobiography of Samantha Matthews, as told to David Shields

Life Is Short—Art Is Shorter: In Praise of Brevity, co-editor with Elizabeth Cooperman

I Think You're Totally Wrong: A Quarrel, co-author with Caleb Powell

Salinger, co-author with Shane Salerno

How Literature Saved My Life

Fakes: An Anthology of Pseudo-Interviews, Faux-Lectures, Quasi-Letters, "Found" Texts, and Other Fraudulent Artifacts, co-editor with Matthew Vollmer

Jeff, One Lonely Guy, co-author with
Jeff Ragsdale and Michael Logan

The Inevitable: Contemporary Writers Confront Death,
co-editor with Bradford Morrow

Reality Hunger: A Manifesto

The Thing about Life Is That One Day You'll Be Dead

Body Politic: The Great American Sports Machine

Enough About You: Notes toward the New Autobiography

Baseball Is Just Baseball: The Understated Ichiro

Black Planet: Facing Race during an NBA Season

Remote: Reflections on Life in the Shadow of Celebrity

Handbook for Drowning: A Novel in Stories

Dead Languages: A Novel

Heroes: A Novel

Some of the quotations in this book have been edited slightly for the sake of concision, clarity, and stylistic uniformity. However, every effort has been made to maintain the meaning of the original. For the complete quotation, please see the corresponding citation/URL in the back of the book.

Passages in italics quote the words of Donald Trump.

CONTENTS

We live in a strange time; extraordinary events keep happening that undermine the stability of our world. Yet those in control seem unable to deal with it. No one has any vision of a different or a better kind of future. Over the past forty years, rather than face up to the real complexities of the world, politicians, financiers, and technological utopians retreated. Instead, they constructed a simpler version of the world in order to hang onto power. As this fake world grew, all of us went along with it, because the simplicity was reassuring. Even those who thought they were attacking the system (the radicals, the artists, the musicians, and our whole counterculture) actually became part of the trickery, because they, too, had retreated into the make-believe world. Which is why their opposition has no effect and nothing ever changes.

—ADAM CURTIS

A RAGE TO INJURE
WHAT'S INJURED US

PROLOGUE.

Around the corner from me in Seattle, Open Books—one of only four all-poetry bookstores in the country—juxtaposes two passages in the typewriter in its display window: Jane Wong's "Tell me, / what have you learned from / loneliness? Whose spoon / do you lick?" and Nicanor Parra's "Sorry to Be So Blunt, General," which begins, "Even the star on your beret / looks fake to me / and yet tears are rolling down my cheeks." It's the inextricability of the first excerpt from the second one that characterizes our moment.

On *The Michael Medved Show* (right-wing talk radio, with an occasional nod toward centrism), a Christian lady says, "There's a sense of heaviness wherever you go." This is exactly right, and this is a not insignificant part of what I'm interested in—describing that heaviness.

ROSEBUD.

In the pool, a professional mediator of injury cases tells me that plaintiffs are invariably convinced their life was perfect before the accident; her job is to disabuse the plaintiff of this notion. Absurdly, I'm determined to figure out what Donald Trump's original wound is. It's not yet apparent to me.

Nobody takes things more personally than me. When somebody says something personal about me, I hate them for the rest of my life. It's probably wrong, but I hate people. Do you understand that? I hate 'em. I never recover from it.

"If we can't explain why a cockroach decides to turn left," Noam Chomsky asks, "how can we explain why a human being decides to do something?"

I like to pride myself on rolling with the punches.

*

ERROL MORRIS: What's your favorite movie?

TRUMP: *Citizen Kane* was really about accumulation. And at the end of the accumulation, you see what happens and it's not necessarily all positive. Not positive. I think you learn in *Kane* that maybe wealth isn't everything—because he had the wealth, but he didn't have the happiness. The table getting larger and larger and larger, with he and his wife getting further and further apart as he got wealthier and wealthier: perhaps I can understand that. The relationship that he had was not good for him. Probably not a great one for her, although there were benefits for her. But in the end she was certainly not a happy camper. In real life, I believe wealth does, in fact, isolate you from other people. It's a protective mechanism. You have your guard up, much more so than you would if you didn't have wealth. There was a great rise in *Citizen Kane* and there was a modest fall. The fall wasn't a financial fall; the fall was a personal fall, but it was a fall nevertheless. So you had the highs and you had the lows. A lot of people don't really understand the significance of [the word "rosebud"], but I think the significance is bringing a lonely, rather sad figure back into his childhood. The word "rosebud," for whatever reason, has captivated movie-goers and movie-watchers for so many years, and perhaps if they came up with another word that meant the same thing, it wouldn't have worked, but "rosebud" works.

MORRIS: "Rosebud" works.

TRUMP: Right. For whatever reason.

MORRIS: If you could give Charles Foster Kane advice, what would you say to him?

TRUMP: Get yourself a different woman.

(He's kind of getting it, he's getting it, he's really getting it; forget it, he doesn't get it.)

*

What degree and angle of self-loathing necessitate Trump's obsession with being liked (not just liked but, rather, loved; not even loved; adored, worshipped) on a second-by-second basis? What sadness animates this need to be flattered and fluffed?

The National Enquirer *did a story on me not so long ago that in the history of the world nobody has gotten more beautiful women than I have, which is a great compliment.*

I do love Fox News and, by the way, they do love me.

People love me. They love me like they love Howard [Stern]. *For the same reason. Because we're wackos, right?*

HOW HATRED
ALMOST ALWAYS WORKS.

In the last episode of (the actually not very good series) *Gypsy*, Naomi Watts, playing a crazy shrink (is there any other kind?), says something that I nevertheless find useful: "I want to address the root causes of bullying and talk about what motivates that behavior. It often comes from a deep-seated lack of stability—a ground that was never really solid. And yet, unsurprisingly, those who have been bullied are going to become bullies themselves. They want to inflict pain on others mostly because they don't want to feel the pain. Perhaps they try to distract you through intimidation or lies so you don't see their truth, their guilt, their own shame. It's deeply embedded from their history, their experiences, even their upbringing. And, lastly, there are the ones who want power because they just don't want to feel powerless any longer. They need an outlet. To really have power, one must have it over something or someone. But it's never really about that person, that situation. Those people who truly desire power are actually only trying to control one thing: themselves."

In my academic life, I've encountered at least three psychopathic bullies; I capitulated to their demands because they had something I wanted/needed. (I hope that was the reason.) What, precisely, does Trump have that anybody wants or needs?

Why have bullies targeted me throughout my life? My reluctance, due to my stutter, to be directly confrontational? What's everyone else's excuse?

Whence my antipathy for the wizened, bald, arthritic, Chinese man frequently swimming in the pool alongside me? What does his painfully slow Australian crawl remind me of other than, of course, my own?

My colleague Ethan emails me, "What I really want to read right now, which I haven't found, is a manual on how to win an argument (or battle of rhetoric) with a bully. I rarely have an argument with such a bully, but in my internal monologue I'm constantly trying to counter whatever new bullshit I hear the administration and its allies trot out. I'm feeling so incredibly gas-lit that I find myself wondering if we can actually ever know anything for certain. I keep trying to picture myself back on my elementary school playground, trying to remember a time when someone bested a bully without resorting to physical violence (in Missoula, where I grew up, fistfights were common from elementary school all the way through high school and beyond). My memory is hazy, but mostly I remember bullies being put in their place by either violence or some sort of public humiliation (someone finding a way to beat the bully at his own game). I keep wishing for a totally contemporary manual on how to counter a bully in which the thinking of all our best minds in philosophy, sociology, neuroscience—even comedy—take on the challenge. Of course, I haven't found the book." Dude, you're reading it.

My junior high teammate / "friend" Geoff (every member of whose family was humiliated by their father and whose brother was later convicted of murder; more than one psychiatrist has speculated to me that Trump was abused in childhood) and I would sit on a wall outside the school and say something "witty" about each person passing by; the wit consisted of "praising" something about each person that was his or her manifest weakness/deficit/disability. Geoff remains for me the proto-Trump voter: defeated by the culture around him (1960s San Francisco), he watched *All in the Family* for Archie Bunker's epithets, hated and baited me for being the one Jewish kid in a group of jocks, dispatched ambulances to my house in the middle of the night for comic effect, called our basketball teammate Curtis Xiao "Cuntis," surreptitiously rewrote Richard Sakomoto's yearbook profile into a racist stereotype. The entire social psychology of it couldn't be more obvious.

Whenever he was ever truly challenged (see his interview with Huey Newton), William F. Buckley "folded like a deck of cards" (a Trumpism; see below), but my mom, who proposed that we move from the suburbs into Hunters Point, San Francisco's literally radioactive ghetto, to demonstrate that we were in solidarity with the Black Panthers, worshipped (as a way to torture my stammering father) Buckley's serpentine syntax and sesquipedalian vocabulary. Just goes to show you. Show you what? It's always all about performance. Buckley also stammered, but it was an affected Oxbridge stammer.

Society loves me, and I connect differently for different people. Life is not all sincerity. Life is an act, to a large extent.

Tristan Harris says, "Magicians start by looking for blind spots, edges, vulnerabilities, and limits of people's perception, so they can influence what people do without them even realizing it. Once you know how to push people's buttons, you can play them like a piano." This is Trump. This is every bully I've ever encountered.

David Frum, author of Bush 43's "axis of evil" line: "Trump has a very shrewd intuition for people's weaknesses and how to bully individuals."

Jonathan Martin, an African-American pro football player who had been bullied by his white teammate; who graduated from Stanford; whose parents are Harvard grads (one an attorney, the other a professor of criminal justice); and whose Instagram post was understood to be a possible threat to blow up his lily-white alma mater, Harvard-Westlake High School in Los Angeles (which he blamed for teaching him to act white): "When you're a bully victim and a coward, your options are suicide or revenge."

Why does no one ask what role Washington State's football coach, Mike Leach, a notorious bully and sadist, might have played in his quarterback Tyler Hilinski's suicide?

My immense Schadenfreude when reviewing the Shitty Media Men list—there's not a person I know on the list who hasn't, in some way, impeded my career. The notion of lateral violence: we can't get to Trump, so we target a magazine editor named Christian Lorentzen.

Francis Wilkinson says Trump has "a titanic ego that is paper-thin," which is hardly a revelation, but the degree of thinness is what I find so fascinating. The clues are everywhere: his tyrannical father, his anhedonic mother, his obsessions with shit and piss and germs and Purell and death and being spanked (allegedly forcing Stormy Daniels to watch three hours straight of *Shark Week* with him when he's terrified of sharks: finally a woman to simultaneously comfort him, as his mother never did, and judge and punish him, as his father always did).

I donate to all these charities, and I would never donate to any charity that helps sharks. I hope all the sharks die.

Trump childhood friend: "He did talk about his father—how he told him to be a 'king,' to be a 'killer.' He didn't tell me what his mother's advice was. He didn't say anything about her. Not a word."

According to Cindy Crawford, her husband, Rande Gerber, the billionaire huckster/subject of a painfully fawning profile in the *NYT*, notices "everything." Gerber is or used to be conventionally handsome and is from Queens. Noticing everything is a function of class warfare (an astonishing number of great writers grew up lower-middle-class in a middle-class environment or middle-class in an upper-middle-class milieu). According to Joan Acocella, when people grow up in an emotionally barren landscape, they tend to think of themselves as not being sure of their feelings and/or not sure they have feelings and get their revenge by not forgetting a thing, especially any slight, and analyzing everyone and everything from an unforgivably harsh POV.

Pema Chödrön says, "Behind all hardening and tightening and rigidity of the heart there's always fear. But if you touch fear, behind fear there is a soft spot."

This is a detective story.

ORIGIN STORIES.

The Drumpf family can be traced back to 17th-century Germany; in 1648, the name became "Trump."

In the 1890s, Trump's German grandfather, Friedrich, whom German authorities viewed as a draft-dodger, leased the Poodle Dog restaurant in Seattle's red-light district; when Friedrich bought the Poodle Dog, he renamed it the Dairy Restaurant and advertised "private rooms for ladies" (prostitutes).

As recently as 1987, Trump claimed that his father was Swedish.

EVERY DAY IS A FIGHT
AND EVERY FIGHT IS PUBLIC.

My mother and father were amazing people. Unlike you [Howard Stern] *and I, they were married 63 years. They had an amazing love affair.*

Trump sued Bill Maher for joking that he would give $5 million to charity if Trump could prove that he wasn't the son of an orangutan.

He [Maher] *tried to diminish me. I don't mind. I'm diminished all the time.*

My father would have blown him [Maher] *away. The best guy, by the way. Tough as hell. Really handsome.*

Trump biographer Tim O'Brien says, "Donald has always promoted himself publicly as a self-made entrepreneur when, in fact, that's who his father was. And I think that sort of hangs over Donald. The Trump family built the foundation of their riches on middle-class housing in Brooklyn and Queens....Trump has claimed over the years that he borrowed only a million dollars from his father. He inherited, conservatively, tens of millions of dollars from his father."

You know me pretty well. Do you think anybody helped me build this fortune?

My father is a wonderful man, but he is also very much a business guy and strong and tough as hell. He was also an unbelievably demanding taskmaster.

Trump's nephew Fred III said about the Trump family, "These are not warm and fuzzy people. They never even came to see [Trump's nephew's son, William] in the hospital [for seizures, which turned out to be early signs of cerebral palsy]."

I'm a really impersonal kind of guy.

Trump's signature looks like nothing so much as a picket fence turned into a seismographic read-out, as if Gerhard Richter had reimagined Grant Wood.

I still remember my mother, who is Scottish by birth, sitting in front of the television set to watch Queen Elizabeth's coronation and not budging for an entire day. She was just enthralled by the pomp and circumstance, the whole idea of royalty and glamour. I also remember my father that day, pacing around impatiently. 'For Christ's sake, Mary,' he'd say. 'Enough is enough. Turn it off. They're all a bunch of con artists.' My mother didn't even look up. They were total opposites in that sense. My mother loves splendor and magnificence, while my father, who is very down-to-earth, gets excited only by competence and efficiency.

I like conflict. I like having two people with different points of view, and I certainly have that....I like watching it. I like seeing it, and I think it's the best way to go.

*

JANUARY 2016, FOX NEWS, OFF-AIR—

SEAN HANNITY: You going over to Colbert after this?

DONALD RUMSFELD: Yeah.

HANNITY: Don't take any of his shit.

RUMSFELD: Uh-huh.

HANNITY: Hey, I got a line for you.

RUMSFELD: Yeah?

HANNITY: If he gives you any shit, say, "I'm doing *your* show. *You're* in last place. I'm doing *you* a favor."

RUMSFELD: This guy [Hannity]—

HANNITY: I been pickin' fights my whole life.

*

My whole life is a fight. My whole life is a fight. My whole life is a big fat fight.

LIFE IS ONE BIG FAT BET.
(Trump)

What you have to understand about Ed Koch is that he's a bully, pure and simple. Bullies act tough, but they're really closet cowards. The only people bullies push around are the ones they know they can beat. Confront a strong, competent person, and he'll fight back harder than ever. Confront a bully, and in most cases he'll fold like a deck of cards [perhaps he means to allude to a gambler folding his hand in a game of poker?].

Trump as the world's worst poker player—

I would love to be able to bring back our country into a great form of unity. Without a major event where people pull together, that's hard to do. But I would like to do it without that major event because usually that major event is not a good thing.

People think I'm a gambler. I've never gambled in my life.

WHAT'S THE MATTER WITH HIM?

(What's wrong with us that we can't stop watching?)

Look at how tiny the photo is of Trump's mother behind Trump's White House desk (how dwarfed it is by the photo of his father) and how it wasn't even there from January until April 2017 (surely, someone noticed the absence and suggested the addition).

In his office on the 26th floor of Trump Tower, a large photo of his father is prominently displayed; there appears to be no photo of his mother.

Part of the problem I've had with women has been in having to compare them to my incredible mother, Mary Trump.

In *The Mermaid and the Minotaur*, Dorothy Dinnerstein writes, "The deepest root of our acquiescence to the maiming and mutual imprisonment of men and women lies in a monolithic fact of childhood. Under the arrangements that now prevail, a woman is the parent who is every infant's first love, first witness, and first boss, the person who presides over the infant's first encounters with the natural surround and who exists for the infant as the first representative of the flesh."

You treat me like a baby! Am I like a baby to you? I sit there like a little baby and watch TV and you talk to me? Am I a fucking baby, Paul [Manafort]*?*

According to Peter Lovenheim, who for several years has been researching and writing a book about attachment theory, "The biographical record is fairly strong on Trump's failure to develop a healthy emotional attachment to either of his parents. Mary Trump became seriously ill from complications during labor with her last child, Robert. As a result, at just two years and two months of age, Donald endured the trauma of the prolonged absence and life-threatening illness of his mother. It's not clear how long she was incapacitated. Indeed, we don't know that she ever really re-engaged with her son.

"Friends of the Trump family who knew the Trump kids when they were young report that they 'rarely saw Mrs. Trump' and that Donald, while 'in awe' of his father, was 'very detached from his mother.' Much of the president's behavior is clearly consistent with attachment avoidance: his powerful sense of self-reliance and near-inability to acknowledge self-doubt; his bragging about his sexual relations; his almost complete lack of friends; and his unstable relationships with White House staff, cabinet members, and Congressional leaders of both parties. Overt narcissism or grandiose self-regard is associated with attachment avoidance."

This psychobabble is all pretty reductive, and yet there is a gigantic ghost in his machine, is there not? What is it? What "explains" him? Is he inexplicable? Is there such a thing as pure evil? If so, what value is there in declaring it "pure evil"? None, in my view.

The "complications": after Robert was born, Mary suffered a hemorrhage; doctors needed to perform an emergency hysterectomy; she developed an abdominal infection that required numerous follow-up surgeries. During one of the surgeries, Fred told his daughter, Maryanne, Trump's sister, now perforce an "inactive" Circuit Court judge, that Mary "wasn't expected to live, but I should go to school and he'd call me if anything changed. That's right—go to school as usual!"

When Trump went to his mother's hometown, Tong, Scotland, to open a golf course, he spent three hours in Tong and ninety-seven seconds in the house in which she was raised. According to Selina Scott in the *Daily Mail*, Mary Macleod was "brought up a crofter [small-scale farmer] on the Hebridean island of Lewis." But in 1995 "her fingernails were a shiny scarlet, the hair coiffeured, her manner impeccable—the perfect wealthy American matron, all trace of the humble Scottish lass airbrushed away. A trophy mother."

A childhood friend said about Trump's mother, "She just did not interact with the kids when their friends were around."

Throwing two Starbursts on the table at the G-7 meeting in 2018 in Toronto: *Here, Angela. Don't say I never give you anything.*

Pretending that *Vacationland*, his humble-bragfest about owning two vacation homes, is about "a mid-40s white male monster staring down what I hope is the second half of my life and wondering what there is possible for me to do," John Hodgman appears on *Fresh Air* and, when he discusses his mother's death, pretends, as evidence of his new-found sincerity, to break down and need quite a long moment to compose himself. The near-genius level of bad faith practiced by this lifelong con artist—why is no one willing to call him out on it? (Am I wrong to be utterly cynical about his crying jag?)

In the third volume of his diary, *Keeping On Keeping On*, Alan Bennett says, "Watching the Latin teams in particular, you see how these are boys whose mothers have loved and cherished them and who have all the confidence and swank that come from that."

*

Wait Wait… Don't Tell Me!, FEBRUARY 3, 2018—

PETER SAGAL: As per usual, half the room [at the State of the Union address] stood up and applauded after everything the president said. Half the room did not. With Trump, though, you could see it actually getting to him. One of his favorite qualities in a person is that person standing up and clapping for him. He was so annoyed at the reaction that he started gesturing for the Democrats—did you see that? "Stand up. Stand up."

HELEN HONG: I think that's why he kept clapping for himself. I've never seen anyone clap their own speech as much as he did.

SAGAL: Yeah.

HONG: But he was right into it [the clapping].

PAULA POUNDSTONE: Don't you think he just claps for everything he does? It has nothing to do with whether he was making a speech or not. Like, he claps toileting—as if he's still working on that and encouraging himself.

SAGAL: So he gets up, looks in the bowl, and claps?

POUNDSTONE: Yeah.

SAGAL: Yeah.

POUNDSTONE: "Good job." If you listen closely, you can hear him say, "Big boy."

*

STERN: But aren't you like me, in a sense? You're the child that needs the caring? You need Melania focused on you.

TRUMP: Well, that's true.

QUEENS.

My friend Toni says that her friend "Ellen is CEO of a large company, whose office is near Trump Tower. Her husband is a lawyer who played on the baseball team with Trump when they were boys. Trump was maybe ten years old when he played on a Little League team in Queens with boys from a variety of backgrounds—mostly working-class families. He was bullied more than anyone else on the team because he was younger than many of the boys, who were better athletes, and because he arrived at practices and games in a limo and had a driver, who also picked him up afterward. According to one of Trump's teammates, members of his family were rarely there."

In his foreword to the reissue of his book *Thirty-Eight Witnesses*, A. M. Rosenthal writes, "Winston Moseley, who killed Kitty Genovese on March 13, 1964, on Austin Street in Kew Gardens, Queens, talked, during the trial, at great length and with eerie calm about what he liked most to do: go out in the streets in the early morning to rob men or kill women. If he spotted a man who was not too large and was walking carelessly or weaving, he enjoyed robbing him with a gun or at knife point and taking his money. Taking it away from a man he could catch off guard and overpower with a weapon gave him pleasure, but it was not nearly as enjoyable as hurting women."

Post-Parkland: *We have to harden the schools, not soften them up. A gun-free zone to a killer or somebody that wants to be a killer—that's like going in for ice cream.*

At the White House, Trump Tower, and Mar-a-Lago, Trump receives two scoops of vanilla ice cream with his chocolate cream pie, while everyone else at the table receives one.

TO HATE LIKE THIS IS
TO BE HAPPY FOREVER.

(Will Blythe)

When I look at myself in the first grade and I look at myself now, I'm basically the same. The temperament is not that different....I don't think anybody changes. They come out a certain way, and that's pretty much what you get.

At age seven he allegedly punched his elementary school music teacher, giving him a black eye, *because I didn't think he knew anything about music and almost got expelled* (music teacher, who nevertheless refutes that Trump ever hit him: "Even then, he was a little shit"). He also allegedly threw rocks at toddlers in playpens.

"He was known to be a bully," a childhood neighbor said about Trump. "A loudmouth bully."

George W. S. Trow says, "What is a cold child? A sadist. What is childish behavior that is cold? It is sadism. After generations of cold childhood, cold childhood after cold childhood, one piling on the other, moving at their best into frenzied adolescence, certain ugly blemishes have surfaced. An overt interest in sadism, for instance. And an interest in unnatural children.

Americans, unrooted, blow with the wind. But they feel the truth when it touches them. An interest in sadism is an interest in truth in that it exposes the process of false affection."

A RAGE TO INJURE
WHAT'S INJURED US.

I was, like, the top-ranking guy in terms of the military. That doesn't mean I was able to get along with people, because the reason I went [to military school] *in the first place was that I didn't get along with a lot of people.*

According to Trump biographer Michael D'Antonio, Fred's decision to send Trump to military school was "a very severe response to a kid who hadn't gotten arrested and wasn't involved in drinking and drugging. This was a profound rejection of Donald."

At New York Military Academy, he won a medal for "neatness." His roommate, who nicknamed him "Mr. Meticulous," said Trump folded his towels and underwear "so that every single one was perfectly squared—like, insanely neat."

Steve Bannon reminds my friend David Gavan, who used to live in London, of "the homeless/alcoholic Irishmen I'd see in Camden Town. A man who describes himself as a 'street fighter' tends to have been called 'sissy' during his school days."

In "Bush's War," Robert Hass writes, "The military is an engineering profession. / Look at boys playing: they love / To figure out the ways to blow things up. / But the rest of us have to go along. / Why do we do it? Certainly there's a rage / To injure what's injured us."

Fred informed everyone at his dinner table that he was ordering steak; therefore, everyone else would order steak. When Donald's first wife, Ivana, said she didn't want steak, she was rebuffed.

Steve Hassan says that cult leaders tend to "have a feeling of insecure attachment to their mother and father. For their entire lives, they're compensating for that lack of sense of self by getting praise and kudos from the outside world. In Trump's case, he was raised in the church of Norman Vincent Peale, where doubt was considered evil."

I used to zap negativity mentally, but now it just bounces off me within a moment of getting near me.

*

OCTOBER 20, 2015, FOX NEWS, OFF-AIR—

HANNITY: Numbers keep going up, up, up.

TRUMP: Hey, buddy, how are you?

HANNITY: How we doing on that other project?

TRUMP: We're doing good. Always doing good, you and I.

HANNITY: When can we get together on that?

TRUMP: In November. Listen, you might ask me if I'd vote for [Jeb] Bush. Ask me that and I'll give you a positive answer.

HANNITY: That's good. We're leading with that. That's good.

Trump says that Democrats who didn't clap during his State of the Union speech *would rather see Trump do badly than Trump do well, okay? It's very selfish. And it got to a point where I really didn't want to look too much during the speech over to that side, because honestly it was bad energy. They were like death.*

In the *NOVA* episode "Extreme Animal Weapons," University of Montana evolutionary biologist Doug Emlen argues that animals' "weapons" evolve generation by generation via violent duels; his father, Stephen (a neurobiologist who has an endowed chair at Cornell and who has a minor role in the episode), had earlier formulated a theory about animals and their weaponry, but without his son's emphasis on evolutionary adaptation. Does the show know it's about itself?

A family friend on Fred and Donald: "The two of them together in the same room was very strange. They were both talking, supposedly to each other, but I was sure neither heard what the other was saying. They talked right past each other."

We had a relationship that was almost businesslike.

Trump's ghostwriter Tony Schwartz: "To survive, Trump felt compelled to go to war with the world. It was a binary, zero-sum choice for him. You either dominated or you submitted. You either created and exploited fear, or you succumbed to it, as he thought his older brother had. This narrow, defensive outlook took hold at a very early age, and it never evolved."

Trump gave the *NYT* obit writer this quote for her obit of Fred: *It* [his father not expanding his real estate business into Manhattan] *was good for me. You know, being the son of somebody: it could have been competition. This way, I got Manhattan all to myself!*

The degree of Trump's obsession with Putin's interference illegitimating his presidency is in direct proportion to his knowledge that Fred's business success renders his son's "accomplishments" imaginary (he would have made far more money investing the estimated forty million dollars he inherited).

PETER PAN.

Trump likes to mention the University of Pennsylvania (Ivy League!) and its Wharton School (Finance!) and claims, incorrectly, that he graduated at the top of his class. In fact, he transferred to the University of Pennsylvania for his junior and senior years from Fordham, where his grades were average. When he received an economics degree from Wharton (a bachelor's degree, not the more prestigious MBA, as many assume), it was without distinction of any kind. (Penn won't release his college records, but his name is nowhere to be found among lists of his more distinguished classmates that were published at the time.) He was able to transfer to Penn only because he arranged an interview with an admissions officer who was a high school classmate of his older brother, Fred Jr., who was an alcoholic, suffered from early Alzheimer's, and died at 42.

Fred III (Trump's nephew, the son and heir of Trump's late older brother, Fred Jr.) left behind his wife and children. When Trump Sr.—Donald and Fred Jr.'s father—was dying, he was demented (Alzheimer's). Donald and his legal team presented to Trump Sr. a new will that divided his estate between Donald and the other three surviving children, leaving nothing to Fred III's family except a $200,000 gift to each grandchild (the same amount that he gave to every other grandchild in the family).

This inheritance had included paid medical insurance for life. Under the revised will, Fred III's family lost the medical insurance portion of the inheritance. Fred III's son, William, needed massive amounts of specialized medical treatment to treat his cerebral palsy. After Trump Sr.'s funeral, Donald sent a letter to Fred III's widow stating that her children's medical insurance was revoked: they would not inherit anything above the $200,000 gift to each grandchild.

Harris Conklin, co-author with Ivan Felt of *Believeniks!: 2005— The Year We Wrote a Book About the Mets*, emails me, "In 1966 Ivan and I went to a bunch of games at Shea in the box seats of this guy whom Felt had gone to high school with and who had already become a local political macher of some kind in Sunnyside and Woodside and would go on to minor hackdom in the Beame and Koch administrations. 1966 is Death Valley, by the way; the Mets are no longer cute with Casey Stengel. Wes Westrum's the manager, and the accomplishment is not losing 100 games. They drafted Seaver that year, and some other names are starting to be familiar: Grote, McGraw, and so forth, but the day we went, it was Bob Friend starting against Jim Bunning. Couple of old-timers. Phillies beat us, 1-zip, on a Bill White laser to dead center.

"Felt's friend had fallen in with a real estate shark named Fred Trump—yes, that one. But we weren't out with Fred. No, Fred had asked that we take the kid along: Donnie. He was worried about the boy, apparently, who had no social life, no 'entrée' into society. Fred wanted to put him among the worldly wise and socially mobile and give him a push, like a kid shoving a motorless toy boat out into the lake at Central Park with a stick and hoping the wind would take it up. Well, we tried to show the kid a good time. Lots of filthy jokes. Insinuations about how he'd ducked the draft, etc. But there was nothing there. I don't know how else to put it. A lump of pale clay with very little definition. Great womanizer later, I heard, but nothing like that was in evidence at this point. We had a favorite pretzel vendor in '66: Wanda. She'd play ball, raise the stakes on our premises, if you know what I mean. No jape was wasted on Wanda. We'd all get killed if we tried that now. We threw Baby-T at her; he wasn't a *terrible*-looking boy. No dice. I heard Felt's friend returned Donnie to Fred with the verdict that it was hopeless. There was nothing we could do for him. My theory? At that point the father thinks, 'Well, if I can't humanize him, socialize him, maybe I can make him into an evil operative.' It's really a simpler hack. You work with what's in front of you. So after the Shea game the father farms the son out to the Roy Cohn types—do the Machiavellian thing, such as it is. And here we are."

My sons were beautiful little kids, with white hair. Eric was, like, seven. Michael was at Mar-a-Lago and said, "Trump, Trump, your son is very beautiful. I must take him to Neverland." I thought that was the nicest thing. He'd call and say, "Where's Eric?" I just couldn't do it.

Does the last line imply that Trump is almost, but not quite, willing to sacrifice his son on the altar of Michael Jackson's celebrity?

SADNESS-INDUCING MIRRORS.

When Trump came to pick him up from his dorm room at Penn to take him to a Yankees game, Donald Jr. was wearing a Yankees jersey. Trump knocked him to the floor in front of his roommates, told him to put on a suit, and meet him outside. Don Jr., who claims he has had "virtually zero contact" with his father since the 2016 election, was so angry about his father's treatment of his mother, Ivana, including allegedly raping her for recommending a plastic surgeon who caused him pain during a scalp-reduction procedure, that after college he stopped speaking to his father for more than a year and moved to Aspen, where he hunted, fished, camped, bartended, and lived out of the back of a truck.

At the time, Mary asked Ivana, "What sort of son have I created?"

*

DON JR. [to Stern]: They both did a really good job bringing us up, so we owe a lot to her [Ivana] as well.
STERN [to Trump]: Do you see that as disloyalty?
TRUMP: Yes.

*

If you ask my children who's been the best parent, I think a lot of them would choose me.

Discouraging Ivanka from dating Lance Armstrong: See, I don't want anyone to take after me. I want my daughter to be with someone relatively her own age.

You know who's one of the great beauties of the world, according to everybody? And I helped create her—Ivanka....She's 6 feet tall; she's got the best body. She made a lot of money as a model—a tremendous amount....If she weren't my daughter, perhaps I'd be dating her.

...No, she didn't [get breast augmentation surgery]. I mean I would know if she did. The answer is no. Why—did she look a little more fat? She's actually always been very voluptuous.

*

STERN: By the way, your daughter—

TRUMP: She's beautiful.

STERN: Can I say this? A piece of ass.

TRUMP: Yeah.

*

FOX NEWS, FEBRUARY 28, 2013, ON-AIR—

WENDY WILLIAMS: What's the favorite thing you have in common with your father?

IVANKA: Either real estate or golf.

WILLIAMS: Donald?

TRUMP: I was going to say sex, but I can't relate that to [gesturing toward Ivanka].

*

Trump shuns Tiffany, his daughter with Marla Maples, because she's not as conventionally beautiful or volleyball-player statuesque as Ivanka. Anyone who isn't "flawless" is, to him, a sadness-inducing mirror.

What happened with the Paralympics was so incredible and so inspiring to me. And I watched—it's a little tough to watch too much, but I watched as much as I could.

WORK IS LOVE MADE VISIBLE.

(Kahlil Gibran)

I like workers. I'm producing a lot of really good workers.

I'm starting to like them [his children] *better because they're start-ing to work in my company. I'm business-oriented. They're doing something. I'm not good before the age of 21. I'm great after the age of 21 because I can get them to work.*

THE MEDIA ARE HIS MOTHER AND FATHER, FROM WHICH AND FROM WHOM HE'S FOREVER TRYING TO OBTAIN COMPLETE AND PERFECT LOVE

(good luck with that).

Trump planted a blind item in the *New York Post* in which his second wife, Marla Maples, said sex with Trump was "the best I've ever had." (This is untrue; she never said it.) *That may have been the most complimentary quote I've ever had. Forget about making money. It doesn't mean anything. That was the ultimate.*

Among many other things Trump has learned from Stern, he's learned to take himself down a peg or even several pegs, in a trivial way or ways, before someone else does so in a more substantive way. For instance, *I'm building this incredible ballroom at Mar-a-Lago, one of the better things I've ever built and, you know, the first thing always is the marriage, but it* [his wedding to Melania] *is also a way of highlighting the ballroom.*

[Before his wedding to Melania] *All these companies come to me, you know—all the best ones—and they throw diamonds in my face like I'm a dog, right? They throw 'em in my face. Guess what? I'm a good businessman. I take 'em, and then I get killed in the press for taking the diamonds. Who the hell wouldn't?*

Trump frequently uses the simile "like a dog" (*choked like a dog, sweated like a dog, dumped like a dog, fired like a dog*, etc.). It feels to me like a clue to his psyche—of what, though, exactly? Did he have a dog as a kid? Did he torture animals?

I can do [billboard] *advertising down there* [in Times Square] *because I get her* [Melania] *for the right price.*

FATHERS AND TEACHERS,
I PONDER, WHAT IS HELL?
I MAINTAIN THAT IT IS
THE SUFFERING OF BEING
UNABLE TO LOVE.

(Dostoevsky)

TRUMP [to Stern]: She [Melania]'s probably the most secure person I know, unlike guys like you and I.

STERN: Would you stay with Melania if she were disfigured?

TRUMP: Oh, totally. No question in my mind. How good is that answer?...I am shallow, generally speaking.

*

When he was 53, John Derek was asked by Barbara Walters whether he would still love his wife, Bo Derek, then 23, if she were disfigured or paralyzed. He weighed the question for a while and wound up demurring. Bo Derek tried hard to smile, but she couldn't.

Melania is 5'11", 125, and that's good. I know pounds. I can tell women's weights. Men, I have no idea.

Charlize Theron says, "If you're raised to believe that your power is good only as long as you're beautiful, then that's what you're going to believe. We live in a society where women are treated like wilted flowers. They used to be pretty, but now they're just kind of wilting. The guy is like a fine bottle of wine. He just keeps getting better and better."

*

STERN: Are you in love?

TRUMP: Absolutely. Totally in love. You have to be with somebody that you like and have a relationship with—a really good one. You know, you lose interest [in other women? in the woman he's with?]. It's always good to be really busy. I'm really busy. We've been doing great. The company is doing the best it's ever done [note the declension].

STERN: Do you really think you're capable of loving another human being? I mean seriously.

TRUMP: Really loving? Oh, sure. Absolutely.

STERN: You sure?

TRUMP: Oh, absolutely. Are you talking about children also?

STERN: No. Forget children. I know you're not capable of that. Do you really love—when you say you're in love, what does that mean to you?

TRUMP: Well, I have a very deep love for my wife. I do.

STERN: What does that mean?

TRUMP: It means, uh, friendship. It meant respect. It means you like—you really like somebody. You like being around somebody. It means you like protecting the person. I always say [to Melania], as I go into one of my many houses, "You know, if any guy ever lives in this house [after Trump's death], I'm going to be looking up at you [the implication is that he's looking up from hell], and I'm going to be cursing you."

THERE IS ONLY
ONE SUBJECT: FAILURE.

(John Hawkes)

On whether he's still having regular sex with post-baby Melania: *The French say, "When a woman becomes a mother, you can never 'blank' her," because you can't disrespect the mother of your child.*

Barron [his only child with Melania] *was playing with* [other] *little children in the Park* [Central Park]—*all little spoiled kids like him. He came back, and I saw—I noticed there was a little sniffle, just a very slight sniffle. I wanted nothing to do with him.*

On the first episode of the sixth season of *The Apprentice*, Trump reclines in his limo, talking on the phone to Melania; we hear (pre-recorded, stock?) sounds of baby coos and giggles; Trump: *Bye-bye, Barron. Take care of yourself.*

[The Hilton family scion] *Barron is a member of what I call the Lucky Sperm Club. He was born wealthy and bred to be an aristocrat, and he's one of those guys who never had to prove anything to anyone. He doesn't try to impress with his style or his clothing or anything else.* Trump frequently used the pseudonym "John Barron" when acting as his own publicist and also, of course, named his youngest child "Barron"—the point of which is to diminish his son, in the same way that he likes to say that his other two sons "were in the back of the room when God handed out brains."

The opposite of toughness—weakness—makes me mad and sometimes turns my stomach.

"It's a Trump thing," Don Jr. says. "We have to end up winning. It's a fact of life."

Asked what his goals are: *I want to win, win, win. Everything I want, I want to get. I want to get the most beautiful women. I want to get the most beautiful this and that. I want to never lose again.*

*

STEPHEN BALDWIN: Have you always done anything to win, even if it meant hurting someone?

TRUMP: I have no comment. I can't comment on that.

*

I love to watch people lose. You want to know why? You learn about people when they lose.

THE FRENZY OF THE VISIBLE*

*Jean-Louis Comolli

IT IS ONLY SHALLOW PEOPLE WHO
DO NOT JUDGE BY APPEARANCES.
THE TRUE MYSTERY OF THE WORLD
IS THE VISIBLE, NOT THE INVISIBLE.

(Oscar Wilde)

That [being a shallow person] *is one of my strengths. I never pretend to be anything else.*

*

TRUMP: I've never had a drink. It's one of my good things. I've never had a cigarette. Other than that, I'm a disaster.

STERN: What are your vices?

TRUMP: For me, it was always women.

*

STERN: Did you ever have 2-3 women in one day?

TRUMP: I have no comment.

STERN: No kidding.

*

In October 2011, addressing an international group of 24-hour cable channel CEOs, Roger Ailes said, "Get five televisions. Put on all of your competitors—and you. No sound. If your eye doesn't naturally settle on your channel, you're doing it wrong. The visual has to be so compelling that the eye will want to settle and stay on your channel. You have to constantly monitor the competition, and if they change something that makes you want to watch them, you have to respond."

During the Tonya Harding-Nancy Kerrigan kerfuffle in 1994, I clipped hundreds of articles and kept extensive notes in dozens of notebooks, all of which I finally threw out—assuming no one else would be interested in what I was interested in (East Coast/West Coast warfare, class warfare, appearance warfare). I should have trusted my gut.

It was a deal based almost entirely on my gut....I've always felt that my best deals were made with my instinct. Not anything else. With my instinct.

Abe Wallach, a long-time Trump aide, told O'Brien that if Trump "thinks you've got good genes," he'll do business with you.

I love Halle Berry's upper body. I think her skin is beautiful. What I hate about her—there's always, like, drama around her.

Should I say "figure" instead of "body"? It's a little more respect-ful. No, her body is amazing. It's crucial to refer to the polite choice and the rude choice and then double-down on the rude choice. The (very mild) frisson is in the emptying out of politesse.

Does Kim Kardashian have a good body? No. Does she have a fat ass? Absolutely.

Jake Tapper, "I Dated Monica Lewinsky," *Washington City Paper*, 1998: "Behind this particular bimbo eruption sits a young woman who is not a bimbo, who is a fairly sensible sort from what I saw....She's not a mug shot and a punch line to me....The night I went out with her, I thought of her as uncomplicated.... That said, let the whoring begin....Her good mood and light manner indicated she had no idea that in a matter of days she would become a chew-toy for Ken Starr....Physically, she was pleasant without being overwhelming. She's a little chubby.... And I don't know if she was riding Air Force One, so to speak....I know it will be years before anybody can have a conversation with her without imagining her on her knees in the Oval Office. If ever."

"When I was about six," Chomsky says, "there was the standard fat kid who everybody made fun of. In the schoolyard, a bunch of kids started taunting him. One of the kids brought over his older brother, who was going to beat him up. I remember going up to stand next to the older boy. I did for a while, but then I got scared and went away. I was very much ashamed of it afterward."

To Manafort: *I know guys like you, with your hair and your skin.*

I never thought Angelina Jolie was good-looking. I don't think she's got good skin. I don't think she's got a great face. I think her lips are too big, to be honest with you. You know, they look like—too big. The listener can guess what Trump is going to say before he catches himself.

Do you like girls that are 5'1"? They come up to you-know-where.

You're all beautiful women. Do you think you had an advantage over the men, in selling ice cream?

Heidi Klum. Sadly, she's no longer a 10.

A friend, whose father worked in the CIA, cheats on his girl-friend because he doesn't feel alive unless he's being deceptive. It's endless, this not getting what we want, this repeating who we are. Jacques Lacan says, "Love is giving what you don't have to someone who doesn't want it."

HER, TOO.

In Maureen Dowd's interview with Uma Thurman about the predations of Harvey Weinstein, the crucial line (easily overlooked) is, "Her father, Robert Thurman, is a Buddhist professor of Indo-Tibetan studies at Columbia who thinks Uma is a reincarnated goddess." That is, will men ever see women as real? According to a source of Mika Brzezinski's, Trump's biggest complaint about life in the White House is that he's blocked from watching porn.

Tim Parks, who lives in Milan, says to me, "They couldn't sink Trump, but they do seem to have the power to tear anyone else apart. [Italian literary scholar] Franco Moretti is hardly a rapist."

How would we know, though? That's the thing.

Twenty-five years ago, Dick Cavett said he'd eat a pair of his own shoes if Woody Allen were found guilty of abusing Dylan Farrow, whereas now a theater in East Haddam, Connecticut, is cancelling the musical version of *Bullets Over Broadway* and replacing it with (too perfect) *The Drowsy Chaperone*.

1973, SF Bay Area: that pseudo-friend Geoff's much older brother (who forty years later pleaded guilty to killing his wife) pointed to a woman who was walking with a slight limp and reveled in the idea that she might be limping due to a long weekend of aggressive sex.

The cover line on the *Stranger*'s Valentine's Day 2018 issue is "Disgusted by Men? Date Women Instead."

A friend on a sexual assault committee at a small liberal arts college in western Pennsylvania summarizes his experience in an email to me: "A woman who hasn't slept for thirty hours admits a guy to her room and wakes to find him 'flicking her nipple.' He thought that was okay because they'd always had a 'flirtatious relationship.' In a somewhat similar case, a woman, passed-out drunk, is entrusted to the care of her neighbor by a friend who leaves for a party. The neighbor somehow manages to be sexual with her despite the fact that she woke at least once to vomit. The friend who arranged the coupling was charged with nothing whatsoever. The worst offender flatly insisted that women always wanted to have sex with him and that the two who brought charges against him were suffering from unwarranted 'afterguilt,' which to him was 'pure bullshit.' There's a depressing familiarity to most of the guys we interview, and few are as willing as that last one to say what they actually think when they're facing suspension or expulsion. Another case involved a guy who took videos of a woman who, unawares, was showering; he was surprised to learn that this couldn't be written off as a prank. A woman and man agreed to meet in the chapel (I think they knew what for) and had sex there. She subsequently decided that he had forced her to have sex and brought charges. Because some thefts had taken place in the chapel, a movement-sensitive camera had been installed in the rafters to apprehend thieves; the video showed quite clearly that she was as much into the sex as he was. When she learned of the video evidence, she dropped out of school, so we had one fewer case to adjudicate."

Roxane Gay, the editor of an anthology of essays about rape culture, tells Bob Shacochis, one of the contributors, that she's heard allegations of sexual harassment against him. Asked to know who his accusers are, he's told that they've requested anonymity. He insists on his innocence. His essay, which views rape through the lenses of history, war, and human nature, is removed from the anthology. (The essay doesn't completely come together, but it's a serious attempt to wrestle with *something*; see Simone Weil's great essay "The *Iliad*, or, The Poem of Force.") His take is, "New boss—same as the old boss."

According to the blog *Visual Culture*, Laurel Nakadate "posted an open casting call for young women in Syracuse. The purposefully crude and shaky video footage in *Good Morning Sunshine* makes for uncomfortable viewing. Nakadate's intrusive camera enters the bedrooms of the young women who responded to the casting call. The women appear to have been quite carefully selected: they encapsulate a mélange of teenage anxiety and innocence. Nakadate further heightens the sense of anxiety by intruding on the girls' personal space and giving them instructions as to what to do in front of the camera. Totally submitting themselves to Nakadate's demands, the girls undress to their underwear—at which point the filming ends. A teddy bear in one of the girls' beds acts as a sign that Nakadate is trodding on dangerous territory. While, on one hand, her subjects appear innocent, on the other hand the intrusion of the camera, the verbal instruction, and the crude video footage situate *Good Morning Sunshine* in a visual aesthetic more commonly found in amateur pornography. Here, too, despite not actually being in the frame itself, Nakadate's body is part of the work: the shaky, hand-held camera refers to a corporeality beyond the frame of the video."

Paula Hawkins says, "What I'm interested in is the point at which people break and treat each other awfully." What I'm interested in are the ways in which stories of suffering might be used to mask other, less marketable stories of suffering. In the *NYT*, Ginia Bellafante refers to "the bestowing of outsize rewards, measured in publicity, for certain female narratives over others, for stories that invite judgments and counter-judgments, nearly always about sex and domestic complexity."

My daughter, Natalie, 25, cautioning me not to add "#hertoo" as the caption to a photo I post on Instagram of a Barbie doll placed beneath a toy gun in a plastic bin, writes, "Mostly, women don't want commentary on this from men. We're good."

Robert Siegel's replacement, Mary Louise Kelly, is chosen because her voice expresses to an uncanny degree the exact level and register of pique that women now feel.

HUMANKIND CANNOT BEAR VERY MUCH REALITY.

(T. S. Eliot)

Whenever, very briefly, Trump is feeling upbeat, he goes in for those various finger gestures from the podium—the accountant's circle, the magician's sliding/missing two fingers, the Mafia don's shrug, the Schwarzkopf aim-and-point, et al. It's a hand. It's a gun. It's a penis.

Trump's omnipresent, long, red tie ends just below his belt. Could the blood-filled-penis symbolism be any more obvious?

"A fetish is a story masquerading as an object," Robert Stoller says.

Slavoj Žižek says, "The fetish is, in effect, a symptom in reverse."

Eugénie Lemoine-Luccioni: "If the penis were the phallus, men would have no need of feathers or ties or medals."

Marjorie Garber: "The penis is an organ. The phallus is a structure."

The enormous and inedible quasi-grapes at Quality Food Center are meant to be experienced less as food and more as Platonic versions of, or fantasies about, actual grapes.

Did you ever see a girl's legs in flats? They're not that good.

RuPaul, the host of *RuPaul's Drag Race*, says, "Flats are for quitters."

To me, it's very simple: if you're going to be thinking, anyway, you might as well think big.

I am the American Dream, supersized version.

SO IT'S NOT
THAT MEN ARE PIGS.
MEN ARE MALES.

(James McManus)

When Trump sat down on the bed in the hotel room and asked Stormy to sit next to him, her first thought was, Ugh, here we go. Afterward, she thought, Please don't try to pay me. She describes sex with Trump as "generic," "textbook," and "one position"—all of which mean exactly the same thing.

Normal. I'm a very normal guy. You know, I'm not into the kinky stuff. I'm a really straight, normal guy. I'm not into beating her brains. I have friends, you know: "Donald, it was incredible: I hit her. I pounded on her." I'm saying, "What kind of animal is this?"

Nicole came over and started screaming at O.J.: "Get over to the table—what the hell are you doing?" She was rough, in all fairness, so he decided, obviously, to kill her. She was really very tough. She came over and really embarrassed him. That was before The Apprentice. *Now that I'm the biggest star on television, she'd be kissing my ass.*

BEAUTY WILL BE CONVULSIVE
OR WILL NOT BE AT ALL.

(André Breton)

The primary reason I wanted Mike [Pence]—other than he looks very good—is...

A beautiful woman that is smart: it could be a negative.

Trump, to Stern intern who wants to be a writer: *People that look like you don't write. I've seen writers. You need to be in front of the camera.*

You know, it doesn't really matter what they write as long as you've got a young and beautiful piece of ass.

Jeans are supposed to show off a body—in particular, they're supposed to show off the ass.

When Hope Hicks expressed her dismay about Corey Lewandowski (with whom she had had an affair during the campaign) being the object of intense media scrutiny, Trump reassured her by saying, "Why? You've already done enough for him. You're the best piece of tail he'll ever have."

*

TRUMP: You really want to know what I consider ideal company?

MARK SINGER: Yes.

TRUMP: A total piece of ass [the entire point of which answer is
to cause Singer and Singer's readers in the *New Yorker* to flinch].

IS SEXUAL OBSESSION OF THIS KIND AND TO THIS DEGREE EVER NOT DERIVED FROM EARLY DAMAGE?

His obsession, even at 72, with sex: this may be a mirage—both to himself and to the paying public. It's the one thing that seems even vaguely real to or about him. A lot of men feel this way: athletes, businessmen.

In *Six Degrees of Separation*, Paul is so happy that he needs/ wants to "add sex to it"; he asks his hosts if they do that, too, and they have no idea what he's talking about. In *Deadwood*, it's reversed—the proprietor has sex with his prostitutes when he needs brief relief from his overworrying mind. Trump is neither.

*

TRUMP: I hadn't spoken to O.J. in years. I don't like people that kill their wives, okay? Does that make sense? Does that make me a disloyal person?

ROBIN QUIVERS: I like that about you.

TRUMP: I like women.

STERN: A lot of people think you like guys that kill their wives.

TRUMP [not getting that they're joking; he has zero sense of humor—classic sign of being on the spectrum: *I never laugh at anything; I'm, like, not a person that laughs a lot*]: I don't even like guys that beat up their women. There's a lot of those guys around.

STERN: Have you ever killed a woman?

TRUMP [still not getting that they're teasing]: No. I'm a lover, not a fighter. I'm a lover, not a fighter. Great lover. Poor fighter.

QUIVERS: People would have understood if you wanted to kill an ex-wife.

TRUMP: I've had women that wanted to be beat up. I said, "Sorry, darling; that's not my thing."

*

"If it doesn't hurt," the ballet adage says, "you're doing it wrong."

*

STERN: You're really mad? It was a joke.

TRUMP: I don't take jokes [again, that paper-thinness; it fascinates; where does it come from?].

*

What is the relationship of Trump's germophobia to his paying two Russian whores to piss on the bed in which Obama slept in Moscow to *USA Today* (of all places) saying Trump isn't fit to clean Obama's toilet to German obsession with scat porn?

I've always had a personal thing about cleanliness, but I also believe it's a good investment....I don't like germs. To me, germs are just another kind of negativity.

*

FEBRUARY 2, 2018, FOX NEWS, ON-AIR—

HANNITY: Let's say Donald Trump produces a memo that says Hillary Clinton had hookers in her room in a Ritz hotel in Moscow urinating on her bed. Now, if that was in [the Steele dossier] and it was not true and then it ends up being the basis in part for a FISA warrant against her used by Trump—you'd be pretty pissed off and the media would be apoplectic tonight. True or false?

JESSICA TARLOV: By the way, this is the only show that I've ever been able to talk about the pee tape on, so that makes me really happy.

JESSE WATTERS: And you know it's not true because if someone pees in the bed, where are you going to sleep? Where are you going to sleep?

TARLOV: I don't think he's having a sleepover with them.

WATTERS: It's obviously not true; that doesn't make any sense.

TARLOV: I think it's transactional. I don't think it's a cuddlefest.

*

Trump's fixation upon the words "transactional," "reciprocal," and "reciprocity"—

Randal Pinkett says, "I was the winner of Season 4 of *The Apprentice.* When you become the winner, you get a one-year contract working for the Trump Organization. One of the rules of thumb that I developed over the course of my apprenticeship was, I will not take anything to Donald unless I can articulate it and frame it in the language of 'what's in it for Donald.' If I can't do that, there's really no point in bringing it to him. None."

I often think of people by the way they treat me. Snooki said, "Donald Trump should be our president; then this country would have no problems." Somebody asked me, "What do you think of Snooki?" I said, "She's fantastic." What am I gonna say—she's terrible? I've got enough enemies. I don't need to create new ones.

Lena Dunham, defending Murray Miller, who co-wrote a few episodes of *Girls* and who was accused of raping a biracial teenage actress: "I believe in a lot of things, but the first tenet of my politics is to hold up the people who have held me up."

Franklin Foer says about Leon Wieseltier, "There's this gap between [his] values and lived reality." Yes, of course, but on PBS's *NewsHour*, Foer, promoting his new book, *World Without Mind: The Existential Threat of Big Tech*, complains to Paul Solman about FAMGA (Facebook/Apple/Microsoft/Google/Amazon)'s takeover of the world. Foer's only solution is to renew our trust in all the old dead megaphones—the *New York Times, New Yorker, Atlantic.*

So, too, see David Brooks's stammering discomfort when pontificating about Weinstein, on *Charlie Rose*. In his early fifties, Brooks left his wife and three children for his research assistant, who's twenty-three years younger than he is; given how common this knowledge is, it's overtly absurd for him to be incessantly lecturing us in the *Times* and on NPR and PBS on some obscure aspect of moral probity.

Whenever politicians whom I don't recognize show up on TV, I can immediately predict—based on how well-coiffed they are—with which party (and exactly which wing of that party) they're affiliated. In *Miami and the Siege of Chicago*, Norman Mailer goes on and on about how sexy he finds Republican women (who doesn't?). Later in life, when he was married to Norris Church, he acknowledged having affairs with nondescript women just so he could be the pretty one for a change.

Jonathan Raban, to me: "I'm skeptically amused and somewhat appalled by the way the 1970s are being judged in post-millennial terms. I keep thinking that Me-Too might not have happened when it did if Trump hadn't become president, with every man involved, from Charlie Rose to Garrison Keillor, getting treated as a DJT proxy and whipping boy after the justified rage at Trump getting away scot-free with the *Access Hollywood* tape [lateral violence]. But I am of another generation."

The dialectic of American politics is relentlessly schizophrenic: Nixon led to Carter; Carter to Reagan; Clinton to Bush; Bush to Obama; Obama to Trump; Trump to post-Weinstein reckoning/purge.

At Green Lake Park I stand behind a bush to pee for a long time. A woman, walking by with her boyfriend, thinks I'm masturbating with her in mind. When they drive away, she yells at me, "I hope it was worth it!"

Does the relatively recent phenomenon of "frexting"—(mainly?) younger women sharing nude selfies with women friends, as a way to combat body dysmorphic disorder—never pivot into porn?

WHAT TO MAKE OF THE NEARLY EXACT RHYME BETWEEN TRUMP'S MOTHER'S BLONDE UPSWEEP C. 1997 AND HIS COMBOVER NOW?

To Macron: *I'll get that little piece of dandruff off. You have a little piece. We have to make him perfect. He is perfect.*

This is what is called "primate grooming"—a gorilla establishing dominance.

I try like hell to hide that bald spot, folks. I work hard at it. It doesn't look bad. Hey, we are hanging in; we are hanging in there. Right? Together, we are hanging in.

Stormy D: "I asked him about his hair. I was like, 'Dude, what's up with that?' and he said, 'You know, everybody wants to give me a makeover and I've been offered all this money and all these free treatments.' And I was like, 'What's the deal? Don't you want to upgrade that? Come on, man,' He said that he thought if he cut his hair or changed it, he would lose his power and his wealth."

Does my hair look okay? It's blowing all over the place. Get me a mirror. Who has a mirror?

Paul Beatty writes, "America needs somebody to throw baseballs at, to fag-bash, to nigger-stomp, to invade, to embargo—anything that, like baseball, keeps a country that's constantly preening in the mirror from actually looking in the mirror and remembering where the bodies are buried." This sounds good but actually makes zero sense; doesn't preening necessarily involve looking in the mirror?

*

FEBRUARY 9, 2016, MANCHESTER, NH, AIRPORT DINER, NEW HAMPSHIRE PRIMARY DAY, FOX NEWS, OFF-AIR—

TECH: Here's a mic for you.

TRUMP: Not on the tie.

TECH: No, not on the tie; here you go.

TRUMP: Watch the hair.

TECH: You need this to hear *Fox and Friends* in New York.

TRUMP: Steve [Doocy] is right here.

TECH: Brian [Kilmeade]'s in New York.

TRUMP: I want to talk to Steve.

DOOCY: We'll all have a conversation.

TRUMP: Watch the hair.

TECH: You got it.

TRUMP: Steve, tell him to watch the hair.

DOOCY: I know, I know.

I DON'T HAVE
A GAY BONE IN MY BODY.

(Kendall Jenner)

At cabinet meetings, Trump sits, Pasha-style, with his hands resting above his big belly.

Republicans maniacally focus on Charles Schumer and Nancy Pelosi because he, with his granny glasses and adenoidal voice, reads so femme and she, with her dominatrix swagger, reads so butch.

Brooke Baldwin, on CNN, with the spray tan, exquisitely tousled hair, acting ability, deeply bored countenance, incredibly low-cut blouse, and perpetual-state-of-arousal makeup (mermaid-blue eye shadow) of a porn star, is nevertheless *outraged* when a sports radio talk show host named Clay Travis, transparently aiming for a viral sound bite, tells her that the only two things (ha ha) he believes in are the First Amendment and boobs.

Could Washington's senior senator Patty Murray not get a new wardrobe, a new haircut, new glasses? Could she look any dowdier? Could she look any more like Mrs. Landingham? And yet there is method to this "brand-building." Murray is the third-ranking Democrat in the Senate. Washington's junior senator, Maria Cantwell, is très chic and utterly irrelevant.

At Davos, Trump sits on a white chair in exactly the same manner he sat on a white chair at his first press avail with Obama at the White House. His posture is for shit, his legs are splayed—his feet point in opposite directions—he's pouting/grimacing in that stereotypically 12-year-old-boy way of his, and his hands are placed at the end of his tie, directly over his crotch and forming the exact shape of a uterus.

IF WE WERE NOT ALL SO
INTERESTED IN OURSELVES,
LIFE WOULD BE SO DULL THAT
NONE OF US WOULD BE
ABLE TO ENDURE IT.

(Schopenhauer)

My wife, Laurie, and I pretend we don't know that her teenage niece uses beauty apps on every selfie she sends us, and she pretends she doesn't know that we know she uses them on every selfie she sends us.

NBC opens its coverage of the Macy's 2017 Thanksgiving Day Parade with an interview of a sitcom's star, Sullivan Stapleton, who, asked what we can look for on the next season's *Blindspot*, replies, "Much more of me." His irreducible vanity and narcissism cancel the joke, which redounds badly against him.

Asked, at a press conference, to what he would attribute the thaw in the relations between North Korea and the U.S., Trump says, "Me." Silence. Pause. Head shake. "Nobody got that."

Iowa Writhing Workshop faculty member Hilma Wolitzer said to us forty years ago, "I want to be as famous to the world as I am to myself." It was meant as self-mockery, but it didn't land like that for anyone in the class, both because we knew Wolitzer was fame-besotted and because we knew we were.

Warhol's "idea of a good photograph is one that's in focus and of a famous person." Updike: "Celebrity is a mask that eats into the face." There is no more obvious marker for self-loathing than narcissism.

"If you worship money and things—if they are where you tap real meaning in life—then you will never have enough. Worship power: you will feel weak and afraid, and you will need ever more power over others to keep the fear at bay. Worship your intellect, being seen as smart: you will end up feeling stupid, a fraud, always on the verge of being found out," wrote David Foster Wallace, who killed himself—partly, I think, because he worshipped "fiction," which had completely deserted him. Wallace can hardly say a thing without qualifying it, without quibbling about it, without contradicting it, without wondering if it's actually wrong, without feeling guilty about it—which made him a rather unnatural novelist but a beautiful essayist.

In "A Supposedly Fun Thing I'll Never Do Again," writing in as demotic an idiom as possible ("like" as a filler, "and but," etc.), Wallace frames himself as a Trumpian baby with incessant needs. On the cruise ship the *Zenith*, which Wallace rechristens the *Nadir*, he catches himself thinking he can tell which passengers are Jewish. A very young girl beats him badly at chess. He's a terrible skeet shooter. Mr. Tennis, he gets thumped in ping-pong. Walking upstairs, he studies the mirror above so he can check out the ass of a woman walking downstairs. He's unable to find out the name of the corporation that many of his fellow passengers work for. He keeps forgetting what floor the dance party is on. He can't figure out what a nautical knot is. He's unable to tolerate that the ship's canteen carries Dr. Pepper but not Mr. Pibb. He allows himself to be the sinkhole of bottomless American lack. The *Nadir* promises to satiate insatiable hungers and thereby erase dread by removing passengers' consciousness that they're mortal. Ain't gonna happen.

Blaze Foley's rendition of his own song "Clay Pigeons" is, to my ear, much too slow, coming across as lachrymose and self-pitying. Gurf Morlix races through the song, as if indifferent. John Prine's version is somehow both deadly serious and self-mocking. How does he manage to pull off this particular trick? How does Trump?

My weird fascination with Brian Williams and his yearning to be smart. A college dropout, he worships every medal and award and prize. He expresses astonishment that a Harvard grad and Rhodes Scholar, Rob Porter, could also be a domestic abuser. Jordan Peele used Allison Williams, Brian's daughter, because of the whites-only *Girls* echo but also the dull perfection of her father's face and its relationship to pathological lying—fired for falsely claiming that, as a journalist on a helicopter in Iraq, he was shot down by an RPG. (Same reason Bradley Whitford, the very embodiment of enlightened adorableness on *The West Wing*, was cast as the father in *Get Out*.)

When asked the likelihood of something happening, Trump often says, "100%"'; I've never met anyone who used the term "100%" who wasn't a pathological liar.

EVERYTHING IS ABOUT SEX
EXCEPT SEX. SEX IS ABOUT POWER.

(Robert Michels)

Marina Abramović says, "I come from a part of the part of the world where a woman has all the power [Belgrade, where her very strict mother was a museum curator and a national hero]. In America, it is so different. We are women; we give life. It's the most powerful role, but we willingly play into this stupid fragile shit."

As an American watching MPs debate during "question time" in the House of Commons, I can't get past my impression that no one really cares all that much about what's being "discussed"; what they care about, above all, is "taking the piss" out of the other person, humiliating someone else rather than embarrassing oneself. It's all unbelievably if indirectly and tediously sexual—Theresa May as nanny with a whip, etc.

My former grad student, now working in Chicago, texts me, "All the men I work with are crazy. They're so sensitive, so emotional, so insecure. Often ignorant. It's astonishing. I love them, but it's astonishing. Pouting and hissy fits every day. 'Nobody appreciates me.' 'I'm sad.' It's endless. Keep it together, babies. And all the women are machines—no fuss, no muss, just do the work and don't complain."

Natalie and her friends—nearly all of whom are RISD graduates now living and working as graphic designers in Brooklyn—discuss which if any of them would ever "crack" and kill someone. They all vote Natalie "least likely," because "she actually cares about life." This makes me cry, not just from pride but also from self-loathing; do I actually care about life? Trump's (and his followers') nihilism is what I care about, which may be a contradiction in terms.

To Meat Loaf: *I think your emotions are beautiful. In fact, can you teach me how to cry?*

Natalie texts me, "I just wanna lift weights and be sad and cry in the sauna. I dead-lifted 180 kg last week. All the boys in my [power-lifting] class are scared of me, as they should be."

A young, black woman, towing her three little kids behind her in Bed-Stuy, says fairly loudly, "What I say goes." The kids know it doesn't, and she knows they know it doesn't. What she's trying to do, it seems to me, is embody and broadcast an aspirational slogan: the black mom and her indomitable strength.

On the junior high student council, an eighth-grade girl (who looked to me like she was about eighteen) said, "The biggest problem we need to tackle at this school is heroin." (This was the Bay Area in the late 1960s.)

To which I, a sixth-grader who looked like he was about six, replied, "Yeah—we need to have better role models for girls."

All the men in Peter Mountford's short story "Pay Attention"—published in the *Paris Review* days before Lorin Stein was fired for "sexual misconduct"—are obsessed with controlling space, but none of them realize that the space they ostensibly control has been allotted to them by women. These men are all running "free" inside a corral she's built for them. The main character in the story is a highly educated, liberal, feminist, suburban mother who gets off on being tied up and paddled. Once Trump is elected, instead of retreating from her kink, she finds herself even more in need of this experience. "She just wants to be stuffed with as much terrible desire as possible, wants to feel it crushing her lungs. All she needs is someone to smack her hard, grab her by the throat—and then she can be right there, transfixed by the gorgeous stillness of the moment."

The father of three girls whom Larry Nassar is accused of abusing asks the judge if he can have five minutes alone with Nassar in a room; denied this opportunity, he lunges at him. This is, to me, posturing. He doesn't believe in the rule of law. He wants his daughters to worship him physically—which is not indirectly related to Nassar's abuse of the girls (nobody ever worshipped the nerdly Nassar, bent on covert vengeance).

Every article that Paul Solotaroff, the buffed-up son of the editor Theodore Solotaroff and briefly my Iowa classmate, has ever written, including his *Rolling Stone* cover profile on Trump, pretends to be critical of and thoughtful about the destruction and self-destruction wrought by the Y chromosome but is always in absolute thrall to it: "You can't do a *fraction* of what he's done in life—dominate New York real estate for decades, build the next grand Xanadus for the super-rich on the far shores of Dubai and Istanbul, run the prime-time ratings table for more than ten years and earn a third (or sixth) fortune at it—without being immensely cunning and deft, a top-of-the-food-chain killer. Over the course of ten days and several close-in encounters, I got to peer behind the scrim of his bluster and self-mythos and get a very good look at the man. What I saw was enough to make me take him dead serious. If you're waiting for Trump to blow himself up in a Hindenburg of gaffes or hate speech, you're in for a long, cold fall and winter. Donald Trump is here for the duration—and gaining strength and traction by the hour." See, too, Solotaroff's sniggering portrait of Kevin Durant, whom he despises, because KD isn't an asshole: "He rises. It's time to leave; he's got a business engagement in town. But then someone asks him if he'd like to see the [prison] cells, and Durant being Durant, he can't say no."

Lisa Halliday's first novel, *Asymmetry*, wouldn't have been published if it weren't a barely disguised *roman à clef* about the author having an affair with Philip Roth, who watches baseball games, eats ice cream, complains about his back, avoids having sex, and buys her an air conditioner. The only interesting thing about the book is the breathtaking and accelerating bad faith of it. Part II, meant to earn the book its title, is a paint-by-numbers novella about a young Iraqi man detained at Heathrow on his way from New York to Iran. Halliday, who worked for Roth's agent, Andrew Wylie, for eight years, has written a book that pretends to be astringent but couldn't be more sentimental, reverential, icon-burnishing, patriarchy-protecting.

Does *Big Little Lies* know that it's constantly sucking its own dick at the same time that it's condemning forced fellatio? The *Lord of the Flies*-esque murder at the end of season one is an attempt to retire the issues in a fusillade of female bonding, but what the show is really about is the tyranny of beauty. Every male and female character is permitted to have sex on screen as frequently or infrequently as his or her ranking on the beauty-scale merits. Alexander Skarsgård and Nicole Kidman are physically "perfect," so we get to see the SM scenarios of their marriage play out over and over, whereas Adam Scott, who looks feral, and Reese Witherspoon, with her sadly heart-shaped face, are condemned to a sexless marriage. The show pretends to be on the side of the avenging, feminist angels and couldn't be more Trumpian.

Two ideas are, I think, still—just barely—in circulation: Trump has or had "animal political genius" and "huge balls." Is either true?

Maher asks Michael Wolff, "What are you in awe of with him? I'm not saying 'admire.' There's nothing I admire about him. But there are things about him that I am in awe of, like the size of his balls. Aren't you just in awe of the size of his balls?"

Supposedly, Rush Limbaugh is a "radio genius." Have you ever actually listened to him, though? He can barely construct two consecutive sentences. If he ever stumbles into an approximate point, he repeats it—with microscopic variants—for the remainder of the hour.

I really don't think he [Bush 43] has much of an IQ. I can't imagine he has any IQ at all.

At a media avail: The fact is—you people won't say this, but I'll say it: I was a much better candidate than her. You always say she was a bad candidate. You never say I was a good candidate. I was one of the greatest candidates. Nobody else would've beaten the Clinton machine, as crooked as it was. But I was a great candidate. One day you're going to say that.

He can't possibly not hear how sad this sounds, can he? This is still a detective story, although the (admittedly slight) possibility often occurs to me that he's intentionally mirroring his base's permanent sense of *ressentiment*. If so, this *is* genius.

Maher: "It's because everything is so unfair. His favorite word is 'unfair.' He's the luckiest guy in the world and he's got this chip on his shoulder. That's what I don't understand. His whole attitude is: when will white men born to great wealth finally catch a break in America?"

Let's face it. I should get an Emmy every single year, but they hate me so badly—these morons. They hate me so badly. Here's the difference: I don't care.

*

DECEMBER 2015, FOX NEWS, OFF-AIR—

DANA PERINO: You know how people say Hillary should make herself more likeable? No one says that about Ted Cruz. He's the most disliked person in Washington. He can't get anyone to second one of his motions. But no one says he should be more likeable.

MEGAN MCCAIN: They like him in Iowa.

PERINO: They do.

MCCAIN: What about Rand Paul? Aren't they friends?

PERINO: They had a falling out.

MCCAIN: A true evangelical.

PERINO: God, I don't know what I'd do if it came down to Trump and Cruz. I'd vote for Hillary.

MCCAIN: God.

PERINO: Would your dad be Vice-President if someone asked?

MCCAIN: No. He's over all that.

PERINO: Yeah.

MCCAIN: Kerry asked him; he said no. That man can't be anyone's number two.

*

In *The Brothers Karamazov*, Dostoevsky describes the patriarch, Fyodor Pavlovich: "He was a strange type yet one rather frequently met with, precisely the type of man who is not only worthless and depraved but muddleheaded as well—one of those muddleheaded people who still handle their own little business deals (if nothing else) quite skillfully....He was married twice and had three sons....There never was mutual love, either on the bride's part or his own, despite the beauty of Adelaida Ivanova [his first wife]. He was a great sensualist all his days, always ready to hang on any skirt that merely beckoned to him....As a father, he did precisely what was expected of him; that is, he totally and utterly abandoned his child by Adelaida Ivanova, not out of malice toward him and not from any wounded matrimonial feelings but simply because he totally forgot about him....Fyodor Pavlovich was fond of play-acting, of suddenly taking up some unexpected role right in front of you, often when there was no need for it and even to his own real disadvantage....He saw and got to know his father, Fyodor Pavlovich, for the first time only after his coming of age, when he arrived in our parts with the purpose of settling the question of his property with him. It seems that even then he did not like his father; he stayed only a short time with him and left quickly, as soon as he had managed to obtain a certain sum from him and made a certain deal with him concerning future payments from the estate, without being able to learn from his father either the value of the estate or its yearly income. Fyodor Pavlovich saw at once (and this must be remembered) that Mitya had a false and inflated idea of his property. Fyodor Pavlovich was quite pleased with this, as it suited his own designs.... Fyodor Pavlovich, though he led a wild, drunken, debauched life, still never stopped investing his capital and always managed his deals successfully, though of course almost always some-what shabbily....Loose women would gather in the house right in front of his wife, and orgies took place....Three or four years after his second wife's death, he set off for the south of Russia and finally wound up in Odessa, where he lived for several years in a row. First, he made the acquaintance, in his own words, of 'a lot of Yids, big Yids, little Yids, baby Yids,' but he ended up later being received 'not just by Yids but by Jews, too.' We may assume it was during this period of his life that he developed his special skill at knocking money together and knocking it out of other people ....He now loved to be outrageous with the female sex, not simply as before, but even in a more repulsive way. He soon became the founder of a number of new taverns throughout the district. Many inhabitants of our town and district immediately got into debt with him, naturally on the best securities. Lately he had become bloated; he began somehow to be erratic, lost his self-control, and even fell into a sort of lightheadedness; he would start one thing and end up with another; he became scattered."

On the syndicated radio show *Live Wire*, which is recorded live in Portland, Loudon Wainwright III, before singing a song with the lines "Come up to my hotel room / save my life," says that he would pretend to be drunk as a way to pick up girls, that his first marriage ended due to his innumerable affairs, and that his daughter wrote a song about him called "Bloody Motherfucking Asshole." Wainwright thinks he's doing *épater le bourgeois*, but he doesn't realize this no longer plays, at least for the Portland audience, which goes deeply silent in disapproval. To describe the competition—at dinner parties—to stand on the highest moral ground, Portlandians use the term "stampede to the left."

THE LANGUAGE OF NEW MEDIA

BASEBALL IS WHAT WE WERE, AND FOOTBALL IS WHAT WE HAVE BECOME.

(Mary McGrory)

I remember loving the BBC series *Jewel in the Crown*, but trying to watch it again—while also simultaneously watching the Seahawks-Falcons game on mute—I can't (shocker) abide the glacial pace of the former anymore. I'm addicted to the alteration every three seconds in point-of-view (married to violence, married to tribalism, married to post-slavery post-narrative) of the latter.

The rookie offensive lineman gives himself away every time he commits the infraction of "holding" his counterpart—exaggeratedly pulling away his hands: I didn't do it!

On the Sunday morning NFL shows on three channels, hulking ex-athletes sit in business suits on a set closely echoic of corporate HQ; we're supposed to access and adore the bull-in-a-china-shop trope.

The Kabuki ritual of the sideline reporter interviewing the star seconds after the game-winning play is a sort of imitation or parody of an actual conversation, built entirely of Nuke LaLoosh clichés. What's the point? To simultaneously demonstrate access to and deepen the mystery. Majesty, mastery, grace can never be explained.

It's not just that I need to switch back and forth throughout the day between NPR (Hillary) and KJR sports talk radio (Trump). It's that the energy I'm interested in comes only in the rapid switching.

The sports-talk radio host, arriving at an epiphany, says, "These athletes are like people." He quickly backtracks. Too late, though.

On sports-talk radio, the host broaches a taboo topic sideways: the SEC has better football players and teams than the Pac-12 because the academic standards are lower in the SEC. The implication is unmistakable.

Even in left-leaning cities such as Seattle, San Francisco, and Boston, the sports-talk radio stations often also feature hard-right political talk; MaxPreps high school football highlights are preceded by Army recruitment videos. It's the conflation and the overlap that do the real lifting.

Despite the federal government shutdown, on January 21, 2018, the Armed Forces Network broadcasts the NFL's conference championship games.

According to Drew Magary, "It's fun to rampage through the china shop when the china shop owner is standing there, saying, '*Sir*, that is not how we do things here!'"

THE PERCEIVER
BY HIS VERY PRESENCE
ALTERS WHAT'S PERCEIVED.

(Heisenberg's Uncertainty Principle)

I almost never give money to beggars, but I give $5 to a beggar holding a sign that says I'M REALLY BAD AT THIS. Self-consciousness (self-reflexivity) is, to me, the saving human grace.

When I can't sleep, I get up and pull a book off the shelves. There are no more than thirty writers whom I can reliably turn to in this situation, and Salinger is still one of them. I've read each of his books at least a dozen times. What is it in his work that offers such solace at 3 AM of the soul? For me, it's how his voice, to a different degree and in a different way in every book, talks back to itself, listens to itself talking, comments upon what it hears, and keeps talking. This self-awareness is the pleasure and burden of being conscious, and the gift of his work—what makes me less lonely and makes life more livable—lies in its revelation that this isn't a deformation in how I think; this is how human beings think.

According to William Deresiewicz, "'Fact,' etymologically, means 'something done'—that is, an act or deed—a sense that still survives in phrases like 'accessory after the fact.' It was only in the 16th century—an age that saw the dawning of a new empirical spirit, one that would issue not only in modern science but also in modern historiography, journalism, and scholarship—that the word began to signify our current sense of 'real state of things.'"

Mike Holderness: "Descartes, deciding to work out what he was sure he knew, climbed into a large stove—in order to do so in warmth and solitude. When he emerged, he declared that the only thing he knew was that there was something that was doubting everything."

John Milton wrote, "They who have put out the people's eyes reproach them of their blindness."

Philip K. Dick: "David Hume remarked that after a gathering of skeptics met to proclaim the veracity of skepticism as a philosophy, all of the members of the gathering nonetheless left by the door rather than the window....I can't claim to be an authority on anything, but I can honestly say that certain matters absolutely fascinate me and that I write about them all the time. Basically, the two topics that fascinate me are 'What is reality?' and 'What constitutes the authentic human being?' What are we? What is it that surrounds us?"

Jennifer Grossman, Bush 43 speechwriter, explaining Trump's quasi-popularity or at least populist appeal: "We crave authenticity."

Heraclitus says, "It's in the nature of things to conceal themselves."

Chomsky says, "One of the ways to have exciting, new ideas is to tear everything to shreds and say everything was wrong—which was very welcome in many areas, because it undermined dedicated activism. The level of irrationality that grows out of this undermines the opportunities for doing something really significant and important. I mean, rationality is a tool that you better have if you want to achieve anything."

A sign in the window of my local Mexican restaurant announces MI DIOS ES REAL ("My god is real"). The problem, exactly.

YOU SEE, I THINK I'M RIGHT, AND WHEN I THINK I'M RIGHT, NOTHING BOTHERS ME.

(Trump)

Tom Bissell: "I listen to a lot of conservative talk radio. I'm not a conservative, but I find that type of certainty fascinating. It's a barricade you often encounter in committed Communists and fundamentalist Christians, Jews, and Muslims. And it's almost always a hedge, a bluff—a way to demand that the complicated world shrink to the dimensions of the comprehensible."

One of the keys to thinking big is total focus. I think of it almost as a controlled neurosis, which is a quality I've noticed in many highly successful entrepreneurs. They're obsessive, they're driven, they're single-minded, and sometimes they're almost maniacal, but it's all channeled into their work. Where other people are paralyzed by neurosis, the people I'm talking about are actually helped by it. I don't say this trait leads to a happier life or a better life, but it's great when it comes to getting what you want.

Obama on Trump: "If we get sick, we actually want to make sure that the doctors have gone to medical school, that they know what they're talking about. If we get on a plane, we really want a pilot to be able to pilot the plane. And yet in our public lives we suddenly think, I don't want somebody who's done it before." (So intriguing—how Obama builds his sentences in order to avoid having to use masculine or feminine pronouns.)

E. L. Doctorow asks, "If justice cannot be made to operate under the worst possible conditions of social hysteria, what does it matter how it operates at other times?" At a symposium celebrating his work, an assistant professor asked him whether he saw any connection between his historical novels' conflation of fact and fiction and an unnamed Bush aide (widely believed to be Karl Rove)'s statement to Ron Susskind: "We're an empire now, and when we act, we create our own reality. While you're studying that reality—judiciously, as you will—we'll act again, creating other new realities, which you can study, too; that's how things will sort out. We're history's actors, and you, all of you, will be left to just study what we do."

It's easy to mock Doctorow for being offended and refusing to answer, but what do I do with the correlation Adam Kirsch makes, in the *Atlantic*, between the emptying out of genres that my book *Reality Hunger* advocates and embodies and the "free with the facts" approach that Wolff takes in *Fire and Fury*? Am I okay with that? Sort of. Sort of not. (Is this my "afterguilt"?)

A "friend," to me, on the overlap: "You specialize in culling smart quotes from other people, assembling them, and putting the David Shields brand on the larger structure. Your own ideas and artistry are evident, but you're also asking readers to give you credit for the work of other people. This kind of bricolage is reminiscent of the builder you're writing about, especially in the second half of his career. He wouldn't understand more than ten percent of *Reality Hunger*, but if he were forced to read it, I suspect he'd appreciate the approach to branding." Wait—what?

Stephen Marche, in the *Los Angeles Review of Books*, says something different but related: "In a world turned upside down by reality hunger, *Reality Hunger* needs to be turned upside down, too. The post-fact world no longer demands, as the condition of creative fluidity, a rush away from the tyranny of facts, as Shields imagined. Rather the opposite...."

Q.v. the ubiquitous commercial for the *NYT*: "The truth has power. The truth will not be threatened. The truth has a voice." A nearly exact and presumably unintentional echo of Trump's "I am your voice" speech at the RNC convention.

Released in July 2018: *The Death of Truth*, by former *NYT* book critic Michiko Kakutani, who whined about *Reality Hunger* when it was published in 2010. Was it my expectation, concern, or hope that *The Death of Truth* would name-check *Reality Hunger*? (It doesn't.)

"Sooner or later," Medved says, "there is such a thing as reality."

To me, that's the key question—is there? I'm against "alternative facts," I suppose, but I'm for "alternative interpretations." Trump, et al. are, obviously, post-postmodernism incarnate; it's as if they've taken all post-1968 French deconstruction (and anemic American attempts to follow French deconstruction) and, er, "weaponized" it into political theater. How conscious is the translation of all this theory into praxis?

As Jeet Heer says, "The visual has triumphed over the literary, fragmented sound bites have replaced linear thinking, nostalgia has replaced historical consciousness, simulacra are indistinguishable from reality, an aesthetic of pastiche and kitsch has replaced modernism's striving for purity, and a shared culture of vulgarity papers over intensifying class disparities. In virtually every detail, Trump seems like the perfect manifestation of postmodernism."

In "popular culture," the word "deconstruction" is nearly constantly misused to now mean any vague sort of semi-dismantling—for instance, the deconstruction of the menu at IHOP.

David Wojahn says, "Fascists, like poets, care deeply for the power of words; they love the slipperiness and instability of language, love the formal challenge of hammering falsehood into received wisdom, just as poets love the nuanced intricacies of turning 140 syllables of rhymed pentameter into a sonnet."

I had an idiot come into my office the other day. He says to me, "Mister Trump, I'm a great negotiator." I'm making a deal with this guy, right? "I read all your books. I can really negotiate, too." Now, I've never met a good negotiator that tells you he's a good negotiator"—the core claim of all of the books Trump has "written."

Trump's misspellings (e.g., "unpresidented," "State of the Uniom," "Special Council," "Teresa May," "Air Force Once," "Marine Core," "Melanie is feeling and doing really well") may have begun, decades ago, by accident, but now they're clearly purposeful—major base-build.

Maher: "Illiteracy isn't Trump's shame; it's his bond."

You know what I hate? Misspellings [double-reverse back somersault].

AN OPEN LETTER TO THE AMERICAN PEOPLE.

My friend Andrew Altschul explains to me that in early May 2016 his fellow novelist Mark Slouka wrote to him "with an idea. Donald Trump had all but secured the Republican nomination for President, and Mark said, 'It's surreal—the lies, bombast, xenophobia, racism, etc., but from what I know of 20th century history, the not-so-slow slide toward authoritarianism is often surreal.' Mark's parents had been in Prague when the Nazis marched in. Later, they'd fled Communist domination of Czechoslovakia and not gone back for forty years. He knew what he was talking about.

"Proposing that we circulate a petition among writers, Mark said, 'It's time for all of us to speak up in any way we can.' Over the next week, we debated how such a petition could reach the widest audience; of course, we wanted some writers with name recognition, but on the other hand we wanted raw numbers, to demonstrate the breadth of opposition. Eventually we decided on a two-pronged approach: we would first publish an 'open letter,' signed by writers, that laid out what we saw as the terrible danger of this turn in our national politics; the letter would be linked to an online petition, open to anyone who agreed with the principles we'd set out. Mark and I reviewed our contacts and divided up the 'asks.' Our goal was to have two hundred signatories to the initial letter. We passed that mark in four days.

"In eight short statements, the letter tried to make the case against electing a man like Trump: his disrespect for the truth, his sowing of discord and violence in the body politic, his lack of any experience or credentials other than wealth and celebrity, his continual denigration of women and minorities, etc. None of these points were particularly original, nor, we thought, particularly controversial. Nearly everyone we contacted—including Stephen King, Jennifer Egan, Junot Díaz [oops], Rita Dove, Dave Eggers, Ha Jin, Geraldine Brooks, ZZ Packer, Tobias Wolff, and Amy Tan—was eager to sign.

"Still, there were objections. Some were unsurprising, including a handful of people who dismissed us as "coastal elites" (I live in Colorado; Mark lived then in blue-collar upstate New York) bent on demonstrating, yet again, our 'absolute scorn and reflexive hatred' toward 'the working-class folks residing between the glamour coasts' [accusations courtesy of Daniel Woodrell; see below]. More unexpected were the refusals from the left: the letter didn't go far enough, according to some, to condemn the U.S. for its history of racism and war-mongering or to acknowledge the anti-democratic currents in American life that had made Trump possible in the first place. Where were all these people when Bush was invading Iraq, one writer asked? How dare we refer to the United States as a 'grand experiment in bringing people of different backgrounds together,' given the rampant bigotry encountered every day by people of color and members of the LGBTQ community?

These accusations were harder to swallow. We had no illusions that the U.S. was a perfect place before Trump came along. It just seemed to us that doing whatever small thing we could to stand against the rise of a tin-pot tyrant outweighed such differences of opinion and strategy. We responded as thoughtfully as we could, convinced a few of the dissenters to sign on, and agreed to disagree with the rest.

"By the time we sent the letter to LitHub, we had 472 signatures from 39 states, including ten winners of the Pulitzer Prize and four National Book Award winners. We reached out to contacts at traditional outlets like the *New York Times*, the *Washington Post*, and the *Guardian*, and newer media like *BuzzFeed* and *Salon*. We learned how to use Twitter and broadcast the content of the letter in a series of ten tweets. On May 24, the day the letter went live, my family and I had plans to fly to the East Coast. Because of the time difference, we boarded our flight before it was published and we landed after 5 p.m. By the time I turned on my phone, the petition had more than five thousand signatures (it would eventually reach 25,000), our Twitter account had a thousand followers, and I had voicemails from CNN and MSNBC asking if Mark and I were available to appear on their programs that night."

One writer, declining to sign the letter, made sure to mention that "in two days I leave for Tokyo. More about that some other time."

Woodrell, the author of the novel *Winter's Bone*, also declined to sign the letter, saying, "A Democratic pooh-bah from Palo Alto, California, visited [West Plains, Missouri—the Ozarks] briefly, surveyed the town square, and said, 'Christ, look at all these crappy, tasteless cars! I mean, look at this heap.' I told him, 'That's my heap. It gets me places, and back, so fuck you very much.' He then left town without doing what he'd come to do." I was raised in a suburb just a few miles north of Palo Alto; the likelihood of the Democratic pooh-bah saying this aloud is nil. So, too, the likelihood of Woodrell saying this aloud.

Lewis Lapham, who is the former editor-in-chief of *Harper's* and whose politics are a bewildering combination of righteous rage and left-wing self-loathing, declined as well, writing to Slouka, "As you surmised, I'm not a petition-signing man, so I'm letting pass by the open letter to the American people. Let me know if and when you need a break from the scribbling away in Brewster, and I'll gladly stand you to a lunch or a dinner in New York." A purer example of clean hands doctrine would be nearly impossible to find.

P.S. from Altschul: "While I, of course, stand by every word of "An Open Letter to the American People" and am glad we did it (even though I didn't fool myself, even at the time, into thinking it would do anything), I'd be lying if I pretended that while it was all going on, I wasn't also thinking, What a fortunate coincidence—my agent was trying to sell my new novel about American 'exceptionalism,' and here I was, being mentioned in dozens of publications; appearing on CNN International; being talked about (however dismissively) on *On the Media*, etc., etc. I can't deny that I felt very clever in giving myself that publicity boost right when I needed it most."

Alexsandar Hemon, who also refused to sign the letter: "Perhaps there is an author among the 'Open Letter' signatories eager to develop a narrative in which Trump wouldn't be the false cause of our discontent but a symbol of an America struggling to forestall its precipitous intellectual and political decline, to which the absence of such a book from American public discourse must surely have contributed."

STRATEGIES OF INDIRECTION.

Why did Ailes, only a few years ago, offer to pay Rachel Maddow, in her words, a "full contract to not work," to "put me on ice"? Because he got and she gets that TV is, in Marshall McLuhan's terms, "cold"; no matter how mad she is, she stays icy. She's funny, which means she's mean. (Margaret Atwood: "Men are afraid that women will laugh at them; women are afraid that men will kill them.") Raban texts me, "I've begun to find Rachel Maddow more than faintly wearisome with all her determined brightness of tone (when I'd prefer to weep)." Do we now need howling opposition, or is clinical detachment more effective? This remains, for me, an open and interesting question.

Maddow's addiction to the phrase "report out"—she's a gifted mugger for the camera, snark-artist, synthesizer, but she's not a journalist. She plays one on TV.

And yet how many times a day do I check Maddow's blog? What, exactly, do I hope to find there? (How OCD/ADD have I become?)

Maddow is obsessed with what my college writing teacher David Milch liked to call "strategy of indirection." She loves to perform five-minute prologues that go precisely nowhere. This is related—indirectly!—to Trump's allergy to staying on script (his need to release internal pressure by loosening an external valve), his addiction to improv (James Parker: "He can't go off message because his message is, Look at me—I'm off message"), Holden Caulfield's aria to speech-class digression, Salinger's obsession from his mid-40s onward with something close to free association (and the relationship of this for Salinger to post-WWII PTSD), my obsession with anti-linear writing as a vibrating vector on the grid of stuttering.

Vonnegut: "Each clump of symbols is a brief, urgent message—describing a situation, a scene. We read them all at once, not one after the other. The author has chosen them carefully, so that when seen all at once, they produce an image of life that is beautiful and surprising and deep."

Walter Benjamin: "How this work was written: rung by rung, according as chance would offer a narrow foothold and always like someone who scales dangerous heights and never allows himself a moment to look about, for fear of becoming dizzy (but also because he would save for the end the full force of the pandemonium opening out for him)."

MOST PEOPLE HAVE LOST
EVEN THE NOSTALGIA FOR
THE LOST NARRATIVE.

(Jean-Francois Lyotard)

W. G. Sebald: "If you refer to Jane Austen, you refer to a world where there were set standards of propriety that were accepted by everyone. Given that you have a world where the rules are clear and where one knows when trespassing begins, then I think it is legitimate, within that kind of context, to be a narrator who knows what the rules are and who knows the answers to certain questions. But I think these certainties have been taken from us by the course of history and that we do have to acknowledge our own sense of ignorance and of insufficiency in these matters and therefore to try to write accordingly."

In 1980, Reagan said, "Let's make America great again"; in 1987, in his *NYT* review of *The Art of the Deal*, Christopher Lehmann-Haupt wrote that Trump "makes one believe for a moment in the American dream again." In 2016, the red hat's blazon was MAKE AMERICA GREAT AGAIN.

Sebastian Heid writes, "The viewer [of *Rashomon*] gets a feel for what could be the true story behind the narratives that are presented, but there is little indication as to what the story really is. To make this point absolutely clear, each of the four narratives is filmed in the same third-person, 'objective' style. We can see what happens, but we learn that what we saw can't have been the truth, even though we have seen it with our own eyes. Because it encapsulates so beautifully the key problem of the postmodern condition, i.e., the multiplicity and unreliability of different narratives, it is the perfect piece to illustrate the different strands of postmodern attitudes that can easily be identified by how they would summarize this situation. A proper relativist would have to say that all stories are equally valid, since all stories can always at best only capture one point of view and there is no objective truth behind the narratives, anyway. We might have only narratives, but the fact that we have several versions of the same story allows us to do some speculative triangulations of the motives and attitudes of the characters."

Michael Gove, a pro-Brexit spokesman, says, "I think people in this country have had enough of experts from organizations with acronyms saying they know what is best and getting it consistently wrong."

Žižek says, "The ongoing rise of populism is grounded for many ordinary people in the experience, 'Don't believe in what the government or public media are telling you.' It's a general mistrust, and I think this is a quite justified mistrust....This is how our entire culture is changing. Today, more and more in our public debate, we have this multicultural, multi-truth approach. The idea is that it's oppressive even to mention that sometimes there is one truth. Every subject—especially if a 'victim'—has the right to say its own truth and we have no right to disqualify it. The very culture of identity politics creates this kind of relativization where you are no longer able to criticize anyone…. Instead of proposing an alternate vision of how to change things, all the left is doing, or at least what they're doing in the most convincing way, is making fun, demonstrating the stupidity, of Trump….All the big problems that we see today—the explosion of new populism, ecological disaster, and so on: Trump is the reaction. Trump is, as they say, an effect and not a cause. Fighting just Trump is what doctors call 'symptomal healing.'"

Peter Pomerantsev: "The postmodern politician doesn't just bend the truth like his predecessors but fundamentally subverts the idea that there is any knowable, objective truth at all. Putin and Trump's undermining the possibility of establishing reality is tactically clever; they thus remove the space where one can make a rational case against them. Criticism becomes lost in a fog of unknowing. Maybe Putin and Trump's postmodernist disdain for objective facts is part of their appeal. Facts are, after all, unpleasant things; they tell you that you are going to die, that you might not be good-looking, rich, or clever. They remind you of your limitations. There is a rebellious joy in throwing off the weight of them."

David Brooks harrumphs that "Putinism, like Trumpism, is based on a cynicism. It's based on the idea that one should have no illusions, be wise to the ways of the world. People are, as Machiavelli put it, ungrateful and deceitful, timid of danger, and avid for profit. Rivalry is inevitable. Everything is partisan. Anybody or any institution that claims to be objective and above the fray is a liar." Brooks's entire brand is that he is that person, but he's a liar.

Breyten Breytenbach: "There is in fact no Truth. We are too fragile and volatile for that; we work with too many uncertainties. There is rather the continual shaping of something resembling, poorly, provisionally, 'truth.'"

Jonathan Lethem: "When you ask me if I'm political, what you're really saying is, 'Do you identify your critique of everyday life as a political one?' It seems to me a politics of consciousness and a politics of awareness are so lacking in most of what are considered to be political viewpoints that I'm not sure I want to call it politics. Before I begin to discuss the kind of questions that people normally call 'politics,' I would have to solve perceptual and mental and emotional confusions that seem to me to so surround every discourse that I certainly haven't gotten anywhere close to 'politics' yet."

*

TRUMP: When people say something false, I attack those people. I think more people should have that attitude. I think you'd find a lot more accurate reporting, including yours.

CHARLES FELDMAN (CNN): What was inaccurate so far?

TRUMP: I thought your demeanor was inaccurate.

AN OPEN LETTER
FROM TRALFAMADORE.

We're all listening to post-rock albums and post-truth podcasts, visiting post-figurative painting exhibitions, watching post-drama theater, reading post-plot lit, and yet we're supposed to be surprised that we no longer have conviction-led politics? We're being told "stories"? The feigned shock is beyond risible. The dissection enacts the very phenomenon it's pretending to dissect. My students clamor for an explanation for the disorientation they feel.

In *The Language of New Media*, Lev Manovich writes, "The database is eclipsing narrative as the predominant form of cultural expression in the digital age. The database represents the world as a list of items, and it refuses to order this list," whereas narrative "creates a cause-and-effect trajectory of seemingly unordered items (events)."

My favorite student asks me, "How is narrative changing in the digital age? Is narrative something that needs to be defended and preserved? Can narratives and databases coexist as different modes of understanding the world?"

She wants me to rail against the database as the predominant form, but all I can do is quote Czeslaw Milosz, who—asked whether he liked Flannery O'Connor's fiction—winced, shook his head, and said, "You know, I don't agree with the novel."

My Republican brother-in-law, visiting from Wisconsin, responds with Pavlovian eagerness to each new media pellet—which annoys me, reminding me as it does of my own hamster wheel.

Parker: "Trump's speaking style is from the future, from a time to come when human consciousness has broken down into little floating atavistic splinters of subjectivity and superstition and jokes that aren't really jokes."

—as if it's a coincidence that that two recent, wildly if differently successful films (*The Shape of Water* and *A Quiet Place*) are almost completely about the glory of silence.

If I don't like what someone says, bing bing: I say something really bad about them. If it's like now and I come up with something, I'll call the girl and she tweets it. Anything over like 7 o'clock: I do it myself. Somebody said I'm the Hemingway of 140 characters.

Hemingway, challenged to write the world's shortest story, scribbled on a napkin, "For sale. Baby shoes. Never worn."

Such is the myth—with zero basis in "reality."

MIRACLE PICTURES.

Everyone knows how much Trump has learned from tabloid media, reality TV, WWE. What exactly has he learned, though?

*

O'REILLY: But Putin's a killer.

TRUMP: There are a lot of killers. You think our country's so innocent? I think our country has plenty of killers, also.

*

—a nearly exact, quite conscious, and purposeful echo of this moment in *The Godfather*:

MICHAEL: My father's no different than any other powerful man—any man who's responsible for other people, like a senator or a president.

KAY: You know how naïve you sound?

MICHAEL: What?

KAY: Senators and presidents don't have men killed.

MICHAEL: Who's being naïve, Kay?

*

I used to want to be a movie producer. I wanted to make movies. In fact, when I was in high school, I always wanted to go to USC School of Cinema. Then I realized my father was a builder in Brooklyn and Queens. I was in the real estate business by osmosis. When I was growing up, I would listen to my father on the phone and, you know, you learn things, right? My father wasn't exactly thrilled [that Trump wanted to study film], so I put movie-making into the real estate business. I've made it a glamorous business.

My father looked exactly like Dodgers player/coach/manager Leo Durocher. Once, when we were still living in Los Angeles in the 1950s, the garbage man supposedly shook my father's hand and said, "Sorry to hear about your marriage, Mr. Durocher." Durocher had been recently divorced from the actress Laraine Day; the garbage man was being sympathetic in a male mode (so went the story). And for some reason I always thought my father stood atop the trash in the back of the truck, hefted garbage cans with one hand, and cursed The Fishbowl Which Is Hollywood, whereas in actuality he immediately told my mother about impersonating Leo Durocher, she cautioned him against stringing along the innocent garbage collector, and my dad chased down the truck to explain and make amends. I hate that my father didn't maintain the fiction, which was, after all—let's be honest—a kind of gift. Or not.

When he worked in Hollywood as a PR hack in the late 1940s and had to greet the director after a screening of his god-awful movie, my dad would say, "That's a real picture you got there." My brother, my father's son from his first marriage and the owner of a film-editing company, thinks every movie company should be called Miracle Pictures, because if a movie ever gets made, "it's a fuckin' miracle."

According to Hollywood film formula, the "big gloom" occurs at the 95-minute mark, before the uptick finale at minute 110. This is why the "In Memoriam" section occurs four-fifths of the way through the Academy Awards ceremony.

Brian Williams and how much he loves to say, "…on the other side"; i.e., after we show this little clip, we'll restart the conversation—as if film were the realm of seraphs.

A Fox News source tells me, "On-air, the talent says the Michael Wolff book is a pack of lies; off-air, they say it sounds just like the DJT they know. It's pro wrestling. The talent is like an overinvested actor: 'My character would say X about Y, would be for P in case of Q, is a family man, cares about sports, etc.' Backstage, the real person is available, unless the talent is a method actor and therefore always in character."

OUR CULTURE IS OBSESSED WITH "REAL" EVENTS BECAUSE WE EXPERIENCE HARDLY ANY.

(Andrew O'Hehir)

Colin Horgan: "Reality TV is blamed for a lot of things, but what it's most guilty of, before widespread broadband access could be blamed, is further legitimizing and, for the first time, popularizing the idea that there's always more going on behind the scenes than is shown. This idea has now become the cultural subtext of the 21st century." Wait—what? Why "blamed"? Why "guilty of"? There *is* always more going on behind the scenes than is shown, and it's instructive to show it, no?

Ronald Reagan is so smooth and effective a performer that he completely won over the American people. Only now, nearly seven years later, are people beginning to question whether there's anything beneath that smile.

Pam Anderson's reality show *Girl on the Loose* opens with her saying, "There's an image of me, and then there's how I really am."

Trump's explicit directive to his White House staff is to structure each day as a long reality-TV episode that he winds up winning.

What happens the day he dies, though? Does he still win that day?

Louise Erdrich, way too earnest for my taste in her fiction but an irresistible comedian in a recent interview: "We're only one huge slice of chocolate cake away from President Pence."

*

JONATHON BRAUN (editor, *The Apprentice*): We went a little further on the tongue-in-cheek aspect of Donald, thinking how funny is it to have this washed-up, five-time bankruptcy guy, you know, who lives in a golden palace that other people are paying for—how funny is it that he is now the 'executive' in charge of this big corporation?

BILL PRUITT (producer, *The Apprentice*): It's a construct, almost from the very beginning. If you were to walk around Donald Trump's actual office in Trump Tower, you'd see the wood's kind of chipped.

BRAUN: It's a mess.

PRUITT: It's still midtown Manhattan, it's still Trump Tower, but it wasn't the empire that we were going to have to sell to people. We needed to gussy it up a bit, and we did.

BRAUN: We were trying to recreate that scene in *Network* when Ned Beatty is confronting—

PRUITT: Mr. Beale.

BRAUN: That same sort of intimidation. I think a lot of people who watched the show believed in the Donald Trump that we were presenting—this character.

PRUITT: I think we all sort of rose up and said, "Now, wait a minute. People, that was a scam. That was an entertainment."

(This is what is known as "afterguilt.")

OUT OF THE CROOKED
TIMBER OF HUMANITY,
NO STRAIGHT THING
WAS EVER MADE*

*Immanuel Kant

AGAINST PIETY.

In 1991, asked by Martin Amis to define "left-conservatism," Mailer replied, "Liberalism worries me. It strikes me as a cover story for people who are essentially totalitarian. They want it their way. They often have one point—a single-minded agenda—and they tend to exclude all the other possibilities. The best thing that can be said for conservatism (and there are a great many terrible things to say about it) is that conservatives tend to have a certain appreciation of the world as a whole. I become uneasy when I find people drawing up solutions, which is, of course, the great vice of the left—thinking they can solve difficult problems—because I think they cut out too many of the nuances. 'Left-conservatism' is my way of reminding myself to deal with everything in context. A solution that works in one place doesn't necessarily work in another."

F. A. Hayek's "fatal conceit": the belief that human beings can predict, diagnose, and solve every social problem—large and small.

An acquaintance tells me that, according to a data mining firm at which he works, I am Irish, a Republican, conservative in my social orientation, opposed to raising taxes to support social security, a gun owner, a supporter of military intervention overseas (more concerned with fighting terrorism than protecting civil liberties), don't believe income inequality is a major problem, not particularly concerned about Trump's "possible" conflict of interests, fervently believe the media has overplayed the Russia scandal, and am opposed to the impeachment of Trump. Ruh-roh.

Alexis de Tocqueville: "Thus not only does democracy make every man forget his ancestors but it hides his descendants and separates his contemporaries from him; it throws him back forever upon himself alone and threatens in the end to confine him entirely within the solitude of his own heart."

Vonnegut on his character Millikan (clearly a reference to junk-bond trader Michael Milken; see, too, the not-so-subtle anti-Semitism, including a shout-out to David Irving, that threads throughout the first chapter of *Slaughterhouse-Five*), who appears in the story "The Epizootic": "I used to wonder what was going to become of all the Americans like him, a bright and shiny new race that believed life was a matter of making one's family richer and richer and richer, or it wasn't life. I often wondered what would become of them."

"Truly wonderful *San Francisco Chronicle* review of *The Use of Fame*. A very happy bit of news in an otherwise grim week. Have a good and safe Fourth of July, everyone." Once a week, I receive emails like this from writer-acquaintances—Trumpian self-promotion under the cover of moral anguish.

It's a tough right-wing balancing act. On the one hand, "conservatives" pretend to be for judges who are "strict constructionists" (there's no such thing, of course; everyone brings her or his own irreducible subjectivity to bear on every question). On the other hand, their entire playbook is pure late-late-capital, post-post-modern, deconstructionist, performative hyper-relativity.

Jerry Brown says Trump has no terror or awe before Our Lord and Savior. The left is now the party of piety.

George Lakoff's famous distinction—between the nurturant parent (Democrat) and the stern father (Republican)—seems correct if quaint, but he's silent or ineffective on how to alter this grammar. Sometimes it feels as if it's simply built into the brain.

Mark Turnbull, managing director of (now defunct) Cambridge Analytica's political division, says, "It's no good fighting an election campaign on the facts because, actually, it's all about emotion."

"Chain migration," "entitlements," "pro-life," and other pitch-perfect, radical-right formulations—why are they never matched by the Democrats? The Republicans repeat the phrase relentlessly, the phrase is fiercely vivid and impossible to forget, and the Democrats invariably counter with something quasi-logical, e.g., "family reunification," "benefits," "pro-choice." Their term carries no raw power. It has no primitive appeal, as if such a gesture were beneath them.

What, exactly, does Trump "enable" in people? Direct access to their limbic system.

My friend Dan Fleshler: "I live in Jackson Heights, Queens, one of the most diverse neighborhoods in the world. We speak more than a hundred languages here. We meet and mingle in the local Foodtown supermarket, where everyone is scrupulously polite because everyone is in the minority; everyone is 'other.' My wife and I went shopping there a few days after Trump was elected. On the checkout line, we saw an old white woman sitting in a wheelchair near the exit, hurling insults at a Sikh man wearing a turban. 'Go home!' the white woman called out. 'Get back! Go home!'

"This was approximately the equivalent of yelling the n-word at a rally led by Al Sharpton. It would have been unthinkable to hear that particular form of venom expressed publicly in my neighborhood before the election. My wife, who's white, screamed at the woman in the wheelchair and told her to shut up, as did a small Latino man wearing a Copa Colombia Mundial jersey. For a moment, the woman seemed bewildered by the outrage; she clearly thought she'd been given permission."

*

TRUMP: Gary [Busey], why should I not fire you?

BUSEY: Because I'm a force of nature.

TRUMP: What does that mean—"a force of nature"? We're all a force of nature.

*

Trump associate: "He is the most present human being I have ever met. He lives entirely in the moment. He doesn't define himself through relationships or through some spiritual interests or concerns. He defines himself and redefines himself from day to day by what happens in his life."

Richard Spencer: "We demand to live in the world that we imagine"—

Trump tries out outlandish ideas, e.g., a military parade, then if/when they get shot down/shut down, he always says he was just joking. Nobody in the history of American politics has been able to do this. How does he do it? It's because it's a given, on all sides of the discourse, that the entire operation is a sham. Everyone knows it and yet no one says this, exactly, because the "right" loves the anti-establishmentarian audacity of the WWE spectacle—the kayfabeness of it; the "left" fulminates, apoplectically and completely counterproductively (utterly symbiotically), and the entire cycle continues, minute by minute, the meter never not clicking over.

A former Bernie Sanders volunteer shoots and seriously wounds Steve Scalise, who was practicing, along with his fellow Republican congressmen, for a softball game against their Democratic counterparts. (Note how Republican operatives always use "Democrat" rather than "Democratic"—"Democrat Party." Why? Because it allows them to pronounce "-crat" to sound like "crap" and/or to rhyme "democrat" with "bureaucrat.") There's much rhetoric spilled about how we're all in this together. We are not. Gore Vidal, asked what he would say to the Founders, said, "'Nice try.'"

In 1995, one in sixteen people in America supported military rule; it's now one in six.

28 REASONS TRUMP
WILL BE RE-ELECTED.

"Just as the worst slave-owners were those who were kind to their slaves, and so prevented the horror of the system being re-alised by those who suffered from it, and understood by those who contemplated it," Wilde wrote in 1891, "so, in the present state of things in England, the people who do most harm are the people who try to do most good."

"If everything's racist," a Latino cop says to me, "nothing's racist."

"Trump is to politics what KISS is to rock 'n' roll," someone says. Someone else does a parody of Andrew Wyeth's painting *Christina's World*, turning it into *Donald's World*. This is virtue-signaling, whose effect is less than zero.

An Australian sex educator suggests that parents ask their babies for their consent before changing their diapers.

There is now a school of animal obedience training that eschews punishment.

Tim Parks: "Liberals don't get how much Trump is their child. Trapping us up for so long in their correctness, their can't-offend, their sense of guilt, they created their monstrous opposite. The #metoo movement is an exacerbation of the same spiral. All men suddenly feel they have to apologize for being men, all whites for being whites, etc. And suddenly people love an appalling guy who won't apologize and champions whites."

Interviewed by the *Guardian*, Louis Theroux says, "For all Trump's awfulness, I can't help but admire his shamelessness, in an odd way. Or maybe not admire but be fascinated by it and maybe envy it. In a shame culture, he seems to have figured out that if you refuse to be shamed, it gives you enormous power."

The University of Washington Q Center SAFE ZONE certificate reads, "I hold myself accountable to: listen and affirm; address prejudiced words and actions in an education [sic] manner; continue to further my personal education around queerness."

Toke Dahler, Student Union affairs officer at Leeds University in England, defends its ban on controversial speakers: "Our single most important task is to ensure that students feel safe in our building. A student union is for students. It's our right to decide who comes in our building. This is not about being safe from views that we don't like. This is about being traumatized. People get traumatized in the outside world, and the student union is a safe space."

Linda Bellos, a feminist who was denied permission to speak at Cambridge University, says, "They think that what I might say [about policies pertaining to transgender people] is going to be offensive to them; therefore, I can't say anything. That is absolutely mad."

Spencer: "In the current year [2016], one's career can be ruined and one's life destroyed if you express anything other than admiration for a man who wants to cut off his genitals and say he's a woman. In the current year, a white who takes pride in his ancestors' accomplishments is evil, but a white who refuses to accept guilt for his ancestors' sins is also evil, maybe even more so. In the current year, white families work their whole lives to send their children to universities where they will be told just how despicable they are. In the current year, the powerful lecture the powerless [sic] about how they don't recognize their privilege. In the current year, a wealthy Jewish celebrity [Seth Meyers?] bragging about the 'end of white men' is the one speaking truth to power. In the current year, if you are physically strong, you are fragile; black is beautiful, but whiteness is toxic; government doesn't stop crime but subsidizes it; white privilege is *very real*, but race is just a social construct; and if facts are too disturbing, you can always retreat into the 'safe space' of box juice, teddy bears, and endless empathy where reality doesn't have to matter anymore."

UC Berkeley lists the use of the phrase "America is the land of opportunity" as a microaggression.

"Dear English Department, We have received a public records request that requires us to help the UW 'provide a list of all trigger warnings for potentially upsetting or distressing content' that any of us may have issued in the course of our job responsibilities. The request does not define 'trigger warning.' The College has, however, provided the attached syllabus as an example of what a 'responsive record' documenting a 'trigger warning' might look like….Syllabi and course descriptions are the likeliest places to find 'trigger warnings.'"

Sometimes the values that reign in academic/literary culture seem completely divorced from the values that reign in the Trumpian universe, but in actuality they're utterly interdependent.

Lorrie Moore: "It's my male students I'm worried about now. They have no idea how to act, what to say. They're completely lost."

The Washington State legislature proposes to allow people who view themselves as "non-binary" to change the sex on their birth certificate to read "X."

Librarian-NPR book reviewer Nancy Pearl claims that after reading and enjoying a novel set in contemporary Detroit, she thought about moving from Seattle back to her "native" Motown. She considered becoming an "urban pioneer." In other words, she would "discover" a city that was founded by Antoine de la Mothe-Cadillac in 1701 and is now 82% black.

In Vimi Bajaj's essay on V. S. Naipaul in the *Writer's Chronicle*, she argues that he was a great writer only early on, when he was compassionate, and is now no longer of interest, because he hates most of humanity; such a formulation would eliminate everything from Petronius's *The Satyricon* (1ˢᵗ century A.D.) to Michel Houellebecq's *Submission* (2015).

The key points of Rebecca Solnit's comically tone-deaf November 2016 essay, "Bird in a Cage," appear to be that 1) she visited a black man on death row at San Quentin; and 2) she has a few more readers for her easy polemics now than she used to.

The moment a Filipino employee briefly enters the narrative in an episode of *This Is Us*, it's impossible not to know that he's going to help—rather than hinder—Toby's attempt to stop a box from being delivered to his and Kate's house.

Trying to write a screenplay with a Tinder addict, the project collapses, because the Tinder addict has zero comprehension that his perspective (he's a straight, white, handsome, late-30s hipster with the perfect job and the perfect dog) matters to absolutely no one anymore.

At a book festival in D.C., I'm one of two straight, white, male, late-middle-aged, Jewish writers, and only one of our photos can be included in the program.

The three principal *NYT* theater critics—Alexis Soloski, Jesse Green, and Ben Brantley—conduct a symposium on the state of American theater in the age of Trump. All are sublimely oblivious of the extent to which they each embody everything that drove five million Obama voters to Trump.

—the American chattering-class's incessant use of the time-buying, throat-clearing, "backstory 'So,' to jump-start the response to a question and to imply that the answer is immeasurably more complicated than the naïveté of the question implies.

In 2000, Al Gore, asked whether he prefers to watch baseball indoors or outdoors, conducted a cost-benefit analysis. Bush, asked the same question, said he enjoys sitting outside in the sunshine.

Promoting her book *The Trouble with Reality*, WNYC's Brooke Gladstone says, "My facts reflect the world as it is. Trump's facts, as a rule, do not. I do not know the facts of his supporters, not really. I only know they voted for Trump, which is inconceivable to me. Which is to say, I can't conceive of it."

On NPR, a woman discusses her idea for a new app, Nutri-Friend, which will tell you, based on information gleaned from social media, whether the person you've just met is likely to have a positive or negative effect upon your attempt to eat right.

The cable TV installer complains about the difficulty of finding a parking space, the convoluted and ineffective process by which Xfinity processes work orders, the clueless customer call service center in the Philippines, his earnest Latina co-worker who wins the bonus trip to Vegas every year. Only after he leaves do I realize he was angling for a tip (bonding between white guys), which I forgot to provide and which will provide for him further ammo.

THE CRUX OF TRUMP'S APPEAL.

(4 parables)

TRUMP [to Larry King]: *Do you mind if I sit back a little bit? Because your breath is very bad. Has this ever been told to you before?*

*

TRUMP: I love getting even with people.

CHARLIE ROSE: Slow up. You love getting even with people?

TRUMP: Oh, absolutely. You don't believe in the eye-for-the-eye?

ROSE: No.

TRUMP: Yeah you do. I know you well enough to know you do.

*

As a young man, Trump was the James Spader of *Pretty in Pink*—the preppy monster. He's now Tommy Wiseau—so bad he's good. Does he get how funny he is? That has never been clear to me or to anyone else, for that matter.

On *Deadwood*, Wild Bill Hickok says, "Some goddamned time, a man's due to stop arguin' with hisself, feelin' he's twice the god-damned fool he knows he is, because he can't be something he tries to be every goddamned day without once getting to dinner time and not fucking it up. I don't wanna fight it no more. Understand me, Charlie? And I don't want you pissin' in my ear about it. Can't you let me go to hell the way I want to?"

THERE IS STILL
ONLY ONE SUBJECT: FAILURE.

In a letter to the editor of the *New Yorker*, Francine Prose, who last published fiction in the magazine twenty years ago, writes, "A few sentences into Sadia Shepard's story 'Foreign-Returned,' I began to get the eerie feeling that I knew exactly what was coming next. And, in fact, I did, because almost everything that happens in Shepard's story happens in Mavis Gallant's story 'The Ice Wagon Going Down the Street,' published, in the *New Yorker*, in 1963. Scene by scene, plot turn by plot turn, gesture by gesture, the Shepard story follows the Gallant—the main difference being that the characters are Pakistanis in Connecticut rather than Canadians in Geneva. Some phrases and sentences are mirrored with only a few words changed. Shepard, in an interview with the fiction editor Deborah Treisman, acknowledges a 'great debt' to the Gallant story, but the correspondences far exceed the bounds of 'debt,' and even of 'homage,' or of a 'translation' into a different ethnicity and historical period. Is it really acceptable to change the names and the identities of fictional characters and then claim the story as one's own original work? Why, then, do we bother having copyright laws?"

As if in explanation of and to Prose, Obama says to Marc Maron on *WTF*: "The fights you have are never about the thing you're fighting about. It's always about something else. It's about a story. It's about respect. It's about recognition, something deep"— which is what makes him a surprisingly Niebuhrian thinker and made him such an ineffective president. He really didn't care that much ("Even after I've done all this, some folks still don't think I spend enough time with Congress," he said at a White House Correspondents' Association dinner. 'Why don't you go get a drink with Mitch McConnell?' they ask. Really? Why don't *you* go get a drink with Mitch McConnell?")

Asked by Prince Harry what he misses most about being president, Obama says, "One of the interesting things about leaving the presidency is realizing that my life had been so accelerated; everything felt like, and still feels to some degree like, it's moving in slow motion. My lawyer said, 'We have to meet with somebody right away because they really want to get something done,' and I said, 'Okay, how about tomorrow?' and he said, 'Well, no; it's going to take at least two weeks.' I said (and I had to explain), 'You know, where I'm from, "right away" means if we do something in half an hour, somebody dies.' So, there's just a lower intensity level. Sometimes that means you don't have the same adrenaline rush, but it also means that you can be, I think, more reflective and deliberate about the kinds of things you want to get done." I can feel it: I can feel his voice drop.

On Quincy Street in Cambridge, I watch Harvard undergraduates who—sprinting feverishly away from campus in the late fall afternoon light—are absolutely convinced there's something worth pursuing full-out at the top of the pyramid.

Probably, it's the greatest thing the city ever did [build a skating rink], *and I think the city is the first to acknowledge it* [that he helped accelerate the pace of construction]. *It* [NYC] *now, from a real estate standpoint, has probably become the hottest city in the world. And, I guess, a lot of things had to do with it. Mostly, I feel, it was the psychology of making New York a winner as opposed to a loser.*

According to Eugene McCarthy (failed candidate for president in 1968 and a great semi-pro baseball player in the Soo League in the 1930s): "Being in politics is like being a football coach. You have to be smart enough to understand the game and stupid enough to think winning matters."

Goals? You keep winning and you win and you win and you win. You keep hitting and hitting and hitting. And then somehow it doesn't mean as much as it used to.

IN PRAISE OF
BLOWING SHIT UP

MONEY IS NEVER
NOT A METAPHOR FOR SEX.

If you ask me exactly what the deals all add up to in the end, I'm not sure I have a very good answer.

According to E. M. Cioran, the only way to understand anything about life is to not fully participate in it. This sounds counterintuitive, but it's actually true.

What I do to get rid of pressure is say, "It doesn't matter." It makes life a lot easier. Do you understand what I mean by that? We think it's so important what we're doing. Especially for us it's important. But you have an earthquake in India where 100,000 people die. You'll have some huge problem going on in Africa where so many people are just being killed viciously. And when you think about it, what we're doing—is it really so important?

Spencer says, "Does America stand for anything anymore except money? No, it does not....I think in a lot of ways I reacted against Dallas [where he grew up]. It's a class- and money-conscious place—whoever has the biggest house or the biggest car or the biggest fake boobs. There's no actual community or high culture or sense of greatness, outside of having a McMansion."

Bannon: "Economic nationalism doesn't care about your race, doesn't care about your gender, doesn't care about your ethnicity, doesn't care about your religion, doesn't care about your sexual preference. The only thing it cares about is, Are you a citizen of the United States of America?"

K. W. Jeter writes, "In the marketplace, rape is the natural order of things. And remarkably popular, too, on both sides of the exchange. When people hand over their money, their lives, to DynaZauber or any other corporation, they know what they're getting. They want to get connected. The customers are always bottoms looking to get topped—the harder and bloodier, the better."

Email from me to a writer-friend who's a Yankee fan: "Why do Yankee fans pretend that the Yankees, with their $250 million budget, are 'overperforming'?"

Yankee fan: "The last twenty years have shown that there's less correlation between payroll and success than we all thought. Big, multi-year salaries are generally in reward for stuff you've already done, and they seem to be on their way out."

(Not one word of which is true.)

Over the 2017 off-season, the Yankees signed Giancarlo Stanton for $77 million for three years. During 2018 spring training, general manager Brian Cashman called the Yankees—in comparison with the even more free-spending Boston Red Sox— "the little engine that could." Joking? Hard to tell. Probably not. He pretended to be joking after the reporters giggled.

According to Spike Lee, the "mecca" of basketball is Madison Square Garden, the home of the New York Knicks, who last won a championship half a century ago.

It doesn't matter what the outcome of any particular game is. New York sports fans never acknowledge that their team choked. They always say, somewhat bizarrely and unpersuasively, "The other team was just better." I.e., the game doesn't matter, after all; we'll still contrive a way to win the meta-narrative. Note the paucity of articles analyzing the contribution of New York to the formation of Trump's awfulness. If he were from, say, Los Angeles, the cascade of such articles would never cease. As a New York-centric, LA-based film agent, who has lived in Los Angeles for forty years and still refers to LA as "out here," said to me recently, "There's finally a culture in LA, but there's never going to be a magazine culture." Is this a good thing or a bad thing, though? Who, after reading a mass-market magazine, does not immediately feel worse about himself?

THE CAPITAL OF CAPITALISM.

(to hate like this is still to be happy forever)

The painter Josh Smith says, "The first thing a young person sees when they come to New York is someone being mean to somebody else, so they just adopt that personality. It takes about twelve years to realize how messed up that is."

New York is the meanest city in the world. It's the most vicious city in the world.

John McEnroe is also a privileged child of NYC who has Mommy issues and is lazy and angry (why?) and turned that anger inside out, commodifying himself by channeling universal human resentment.

Joel Drucker: "We all have conflicts within us that we mostly work to repress, but McEnroe has long been given a forum in which to express his hostility and anger—good business for so many. He hates that, too, which fuels more anger."

O'Brien: "Trump has always seen New York (Manhattan, in particular) as a piggy bank and as a stage."

In New York City, Trump's name is on 17 buildings, of which he owns five.

Derek Jeter to Bush 43, who was pacing nervously a few minutes before he had to throw out the first pitch at Yankee Stadium seven weeks after 9/11, "Don't fuck it up. New York hates pussies"— what, in NYC, passes for wit, when it's just Jeter building brand (grace under pressure, etc.).

David Letterman, explaining why he liked having boxing promoter Don King as a guest on his show, said, "He knew he wasn't selling the steak. He was selling the sizzle." This is why Letterman's show would open with "From New York City, the greatest city in the world"; Letterman hated (pretended to hate?) all hype, though most people took this paean seriously.

Especially since 9/11, New York City has been used, ceaselessly, by its resident publicists as a kind of club with which to beat other regions into prone position.

Lucinda Williams: "I fucking hate fucking New York."

THE WISDOM OF CROWDS.

(James Surowiecki)

Everyone on the streets in New York strikes me as zombie-like. They're all checking their phone every thirty seconds. (Harris: "The average person checks his phone 150 times a day. Why do we do this? Are we making 150 conscious choices? Instead of viewing the world in terms of availability of choices, we should view the world in terms of friction required to enact choices.") We won. We won. The West Coast has colonized the world. And yet what have we won? More to the point, What have I won? I'm checking my phone at least as often as they are.

I'm so disappointed to discover that the phonological history of Spanish coronal fricatives doesn't support the legend that the entire populace has been speaking with a lisp for five hundred years to make King Philip feel less freakish and less lonely. I love seeing proof of herd behavior.

When people shake hands with each other, I can sometimes feel, very viscerally, the ancient lineage of this ritual to indicate that one is not carrying a gun. And yet the ritual persists. Only in America? In other cultures, do people shake hands quite as frequently?

Once, I saw this guy on a bridge about to jump. I said, "Don't do it!" He said, "Nobody loves me." I said, "God loves you. Do you believe in God?" He said, "Yes." I said, "Are you a Christian or a Jew?" He said, "A Christian." I said, "Me, too! Protestant or Catholic?" He said, "Protestant." I said, "Me, too! What franchise?" He said, "Baptist." I said, "Me, too! Northern Baptist or Southern Baptist?" He said, "Northern Baptist." I said, "Me, too! Northern Conservative Baptist or Northern Liberal Baptist?" He said, "Northern Conservative Baptist." I said, "Me, too! Northern Conservative Baptist Great Lakes Region or Northern Conservative Baptist Eastern Region?" He said, "Northern Conservative Baptist Great Lakes Region." I said, "Me, too! Northern Conservative Baptist Great Lakes Region Council of 1879 or Northern Conservative Baptist Great Lakes Region Council of 1912?" He said, "Northern Conservative Baptist Great Lakes Region Council of 1912." I said, "Die, heretic!" and pushed him over. (Emo Phillips is obsessed with claiming this as his joke; he won't yield his individuality to the larger group.)

QUEENS, AGAIN.

In 1969, when running for mayor of New York City, the newspaper columnist Jimmy Breslin joked, "If elected, I'll go to Queens"—that is, to the back of beyond. Will Trump ever, ever get over his sense of outsiderness, his obsession with reciprocity, his perceived need to get his fair share?

When Trump stops at the top of the stairs to Air Force One, turns around, and juts out his chin, he reminds me, uncannily, of my college friend Jonathan Wexler, big man on campus and Rhodes Scholar, who is from Rego Park, Queens. Is it something disseminated via the borough's drinking water?

Can everyone not see through Trump's frontin'—the mook-chin, the Queens chin, the pseudo-tough-guy chin, the glass chin, the faux-black, faux-Italian toughness? He's about as tough as I am.

John Skoyles, who is also from Queens, emails me, "I have to say that during the Republican debates, I was pulling for Trump—mainly because I thought he would be a disaster and lose overwhelmingly to Hillary—but also because I found the totally inappropriate name-calling, smirking, etc., very familiar."

Don't say you're tough. You know what the worst thing is? People that say they're tough. 'Cause usually the people that say they're tough are the least tough, okay? So don't say you're tough.

Obama: "Someone once said that every man is trying to either live up to his father's expectations or make up for his father's mistakes, and I suppose that may explain my particular malady as well as anything else." Obama is, obviously, the latter (although, predictably, he pretends to be both). So am I (the latter).

My mother would often say to me, "If you keep going in this direction, you're going to wind up like your father." My shrink could barely believe she said this once, let alone dozens of times. Same shrink (too easy, but still): "Emotionally, your mother raped you all." When people speak of maternal nourishment or paternal authority, I literally have no idea what they're talking about. My mother was a terrifying figure of Olympian hauteur and disdain; my father was a severe manic-depressive and ECT devotee who was in and out of mental hospitals his entire adult life. His role wasn't to be a caretaker; it was to be cared for (my mother called this the "tyranny of the weak"). He occasionally liked to say, in his sharp Brooklyn accent, virtually under his breath, to my mother, "Shaddup." Once, early in their marriage, he apparently shoved her; my mother never stopped alluding to this moment when, very briefly, their roles got reversed.

Nicholas Montemarano, who was born in Brooklyn, raised in Queens, and has written a *roman à clef* about John Edwards, says, "Most of the bullies I encountered growing up in Queens were of the Trump variety: their words were often worse than anything they actually did. They postured; they threatened; they demeaned. Many were tough, but what mattered more was that they seemed so....Trump's policies and public persona, his crass statements and bullying demeanor, must certainly betray who he is—but only part of who he is. The storyteller in me can't believe that what we see and hear is all there is to Donald Trump. At times, he seems not to have an inner life. This is a man who doesn't even ask forgiveness from the God he says he believes in. He's a man I can't imagine shedding a tear. And for all these reasons, I'm that much more compelled by him." Exactly. His emptiness is galvanizing.

A graduate student from Queens tells me at length how amusing he finds the way in which Seattleites "dwell" in their houses. I'm not sure what this means; I just know I'm deeply offended. I don't want to dwell anywhere, exactly. I just want to run around saying "No! in thunder" (which Herman Melville said Nathaniel Hawthorne did; as with most blurbs, the blurber was not-so-secretly talking about himself).

I stumble and fall to the sidewalk, injuring my shoulder and shouting out in intense if brief agony. No one stops to ask if I'm okay. Such an inquiry would seem "invasive." For nearly thirty years now I've lived in Seattle, which I despise with every fiber of my being.

LIFE IS ELSEWHERE.

(Milan Kundera)

For a week, a woman lived in her minivan outside our house in Wallingford, a (no-longer?)-shabby-genteel neighborhood in Seattle, fencing stolen goods. When the police forced her to leave (I called the cops, despite Laurie asking me not to, for fear of reprisal), she gleefully poured all her garbage onto our lawn—all that revenge upon the perceived comforts of (my) middle-class life.

Two beggars, a couple, always pretend to be reading, but they're not reading; they're always reading the same page of the same book. They know this neighborhood is populated disproportionately by professors and students. I resent the couple's insidious appeal to our higher impulses.

Orwell writes about the poor, "The basis of their diet, therefore, is white bread and margarine, corned beef, sugared tea, and potatoes—an appalling diet. Would it not be better if they spent more money on wholesome things like oranges and wholemeal bread or if they even, like the writer of the letter to the New Statesman, saved on fuel and ate their carrots raw? Yes, it would, but the point is that no ordinary human being is ever going to do such a thing. The ordinary human being would sooner starve than live on brown bread and raw carrots. And the peculiar evil is that the less money you have, the less inclined you feel to spend it on wholesome food."

Asked about appearing in a farmer outfit at the Emmys in 2005: *I didn't even know what overalls were. I said, What the hell is that? I said, I hope it doesn't make me look fat.*

Finally, it's not even that complicated: bread for the rich; circuses for the poor.

Neal Urwitz, Director of External Relations for the Center for New American Security, writes "a parody in one act" for *USA Today* in which Hannity, Limbaugh, Chris Wallace, and Alex Jones discuss the political advantages that Republicans would gain if North Korea were to nuke Seattle. What couldn't be more self-evident is that, to the Director of External Relations for the Center for New American Security, Seattle already doesn't exist.

We sit in our buildings overlooking Manhattan. We don't know— maybe in its own way… we don't know the real world [before deciding to change tracks, he appears to be about to say, "maybe in its own way this isn't the real world"]. *The Coast Guard are great people.*

To a Seattle sportswriter at a Lake Tahoe celebrity golf tournament: *Say hello to Bill Gates for me, will ya?*

The novelist Rikki Ducornet and I give a reading in Seattle to support a literary magazine, but before the event starts the magazine announces, with utterly blithe condescension, "This is the fifth reading in *Conjunctions'* Cities Series, which has helped the journal break free of the bonds of the East Coast literary scene and to [sic] hold events all across the country, bringing its contributors and readers into America's invaluable indie bookstores and celebrating the tremendous regional diversity of the authors and audiences that make up the *Conjunctions* community." The event hasn't even started and it's already been rendered beside-the-point.

Jim Warren, D.C. correspondent for the *Chicago Sun-Times*, asked by Brian Williams to articulate the value of the inside-baseball media blather in which they're engaging, actually says, without irony or embarrassment, that he hopes a little bit of his knowledge and wisdom will rub off on people "out in the heartland, in Portland and Albuquerque."

Wait—what? *Portland?* Joan Didion, unable to wake herself from a stupor of patriotic fervor post-9/11, needed "an encounter with an America apparently immune to conventional wisdom. The people to whom I was listening—in San Francisco and Los Angeles and Portland and Seattle—were making connections that I, in my numbed condition, had not yet thought to make: connections between political processes and what had happened on September 11, connections between our political life and the shape our reaction would take and was in fact already taking."

The "national media" treat natural disasters in Puerto Rico and California, as opposed to those in Texas and Florida, with very nearly self-parodic lack of interest. I'll never forget Cokie Roberts lambasting Obama for going to Hawaii on vacation in the summer of 2010: "It just does not make any sense whatsoever. I know his grandmother lives in Hawaii and I know Hawaii is a state, but it has the look of him going off to some sort of foreign, exotic place. If he's going to take a vacation at this time, he should be, you know, in Myrtle Beach." So, too, Roberts—the wife of a former D.C. correspondent for the *NYT* and the daughter of a congressman who was a member of the Warren Commission—asked on *Wait Wait... Don't Tell Me!* to say something "humanizing" about George Will—said that when his flight from Minneapolis was canceled due to snow, he caught a cab into downtown St. Paul and bought a Jaguar in order to drive back to D.C.

On MSNBC, Andrea Mitchell, briefly surveying the destruction and death caused by fires in southern California, can barely mask (actually, can't mask) her impatience to return to the hard reality of speculation about D.C. goings-on.

IN PRAISE OF BLOWING SHIT UP.

The earth is called the earth because, in ancient German, "erde" means "soil" or "dirt....Heidegger's *Being and Time*: German hatred of Jewish rootlessness....Blood and soil: Trump-people actually work where they live, as opposed to in the cloud somewhere....Lord Buckley's epitaph: "He stomped the terra," which Hunter S. Thompson then reclaimed as his own....Trump's irreducible physicality compared to, say, Hillary's anhedonia ....When a journalist-friend dropped acid right before Trump's speech at the RNC convention in Cleveland in 2016, she saw with absolute certainty that Trump would win; when she did the same thing at Obama's 2012 convention speech, she felt absolutely nothing.

According to Thelonious Monk, "The genius is the one that is most like himself."

Which is or was precisely Hillary's problem. Inevitably, her intimates claim that in private she's a veritable riot grrrl, but at least in public she still, at 70, doesn't appear to have the faintest idea who she is. Whenever she walks on any stage, she installs that weirdly rictus smile and executes that weirdly robotic hand-wave.

As Barbara Kruger wrote, in her 1992 paean to Howard Stern, "Creeps are wound neat and tight and seldom say what they mean or mean what they say. Always busy plotting, strategizing, and working the angles, they know there's no such thing as paranoia, because everything you suspect might be happening is actually happening. And they make it happen. There's no noise, no candor, just the cool hum of retentive calculation. But from assholes you always know what to expect. Because they thrive on transgression, their brashness becomes both fun and predictable. They'll never betray you because they never say anything behind your back that they haven't already said to your face. Every thought is deemed right enough to be spoken, every opinion real enough to be fact, every shit sweet enough to be bronzed."

In lower Manhattan, at my bookstore Q&A with a magazine editor, he pouts when I mention to the audience that I met him when he worked in TV in LA. He's writing a book about Nietzsche; when, during dinner, I ask—in my usual undermining way—what gap if any his book fills in the wake of so many great recent books about Nietzsche (whom I worship), he pouts again. He doesn't get that the "business of literature" isn't to be an anodyne part of the overall conversation; it is, as Richard Nash says, to "blow shit up."

James Camp, reviewing Jonathan Dee's novel *The Locals*, writes, "The locals slouched through their turns in his [hedge-fund billionaire Philip Hadi's] 'country-bumpkin theme park,' and it leaves them 'terrified of losing a life' they 'couldn't defend and didn't really enjoy.' Without quite agreeing to it, they've become clowns. Their suffering is real, but their world is fake. You can see why they wanted to blow it up."

"They make fun of his hair; they make fun of the color of his skin; they make fun of the way he talks—he's from Queens, not from Manhattan. They make fun of that long tie he wears. They make fun of his taste for McDonald's. What I don't think they realize is that out here in Arkansas and the heartland and the places that made a difference in that election, like Michigan and Wisconsin, when we hear that kind of ridicule, we hear them making fun of the way *we* look, and the way *we* talk, and the way *we* think." (Tom Cotton, Arkansas senator, who has BA and JD degrees from Harvard)

LIFE, EVEN MORE ELSEWHERE.

Laurie and I drive to Mt. Baker, two hours north of Seattle, so she can ski and I can...do whatever. In the recreation center of the complex in which we're staying, the paterfamilias teaches his teenage son and daughter how to play billiards, relentlessly humiliating the son and sexualizing the daughter. His wife sits on the couch, looking bored. I pretend to be reading, but I'm rapt.

In their Bunyanesque boots, skiers parade around the ski lodge at Mt. Baker with ludicrous grandiosity; Laurie explains to me that it's the only way one can walk in these boots, with a kind of galumphing clomping, but I don't believe it.

The waitress at Chair 9, the bar just down the road from the condo, points to the book I'm reading and asks, "*The Making of Donald Trump*—is that new?"
    Me: "Old. Reissued, I think." (TMI?)
    Waitress: "Good idea." (To read such a book, I think.)
    We're circling each other warily. Such is my gloss, given the escalating popularity of TRUMP signs on the drive up from Seattle; nearby Whatcom County was evenly split in the primaries between Trump and Bernie.

Three Billboards Outside Ebbing, Missouri scores innumerable points against the rednecks it pretends to be interested in portraying. Martin McDonagh doesn't have the slightest interest in understanding hatred. He wants to condescend to it and then be congratulated for granting it the benediction of his faux-wisdom. Great title, though. Cool camerawork.

IN PRAISE OF
NOT GIVING A FUCK.

On *The Ellen DeGeneres Show*, Michelle Obama says, "Forget what they're saying in Washington"—that is, go on with your lives as before. The audience applauds at length.

Upon being informed that he has won the 2017 Nobel Prize in Literature, Kazuo Ishiguro's advice to himself and his fellow writers is to ignore Trump and just get on with one's own work, as this is the way civilization continues. Does he have a clue how closely he's echoing the supposedly contemptible narrator of *The Remains of the Day*?

Under the guise of anti-Blair rhetoric, Bennett's *Keeping On Keeping On* is in deep thrall to the diarist-playwright's middle-brow success. This may be my own overemphasis, of course; I find "success" utterly irrelevant (Updike: "If temporality is held to be invalidating, then nothing real succeeds"). I want to write a play set in Stockholm during the week of parties leading up to a poet receiving the Nobel Prize in Literature, and the poet thinking very little of his own life and work.

In *Summertime*, J. M. Coetzee gives these words to a fictional interviewee, Sophie, to say about himself (and in context the implication is that he believes them): "You do not sense you are in the presence of a writer who is deforming his medium in order to say what has never been said before, which is to me the mark of great writing."

I've always liked Toni Morrison's parenthetical ode, in an interview somewhere, to black men who spend their days perched on porch steps, gleefully giving up.

I watch late-middle-aged black ladies, working in the kitchen of a Tallahassee hotel the morning after Trump's first State of the Union address, listen to a religious show on the radio and glide through their chores in a beautiful haze (they can't be touched).

Horrific book but great title: *The Subtle Art of Not Giving a Fuck.*

EVERY ACT OF CREATION IS
FIRST AN ACT OF DESTRUCTION.

(Picasso)

Whence the origin of the uniquely American phenomenon of the TV and/or radio host welcoming the correspondent, the correspondent expressing his or her delight at being welcomed, the host thanking the correspondent for delivering his or her report, and then the correspondent thanking the host for allowing him or her to deliver it? The point, I think, is that the report finally doesn't matter; what matters is that we're all getting along incredibly well; far and away the worst are Tamara Keith and Domenico Montanaro, who, if informing the NPR and/or PBS audience that WWIII had started, would still be pleading for our twinkly approval.

Anything—anything—is better than NPR's onesy-twosy earnestness. I literally can't listen to it anymore.

Anything—anything—is more appealing than Ari Shapiro's instantaneous, ersatz empathy on NPR. This is where Trump comes in—

—the pitiful veneer of "genteel society" that he has gleefully ripped away, how full of shit so many people on the left are, not because they're wrong per se but because they're so committed to an Oprah-ized, airbrushed, focus-grouped, ultimately empty language in which they can't convince anyone of anything anymore. For me, the absolute avatar of this is John Kerry, who hasn't spoken a word from his heart/gut since those 1971 Congressional hearings. "Liberals"—who won't call, er, a spade a spade—reduce even the most urgent political issue (e.g., health care, gun control, etc.) to soggy politesse and etiquette and meaningless word packages. This is why they always lose; as Altschul says, they're playing badminton, and the Republicans are playing ice hockey. It's enough to make us wish someone would come along and just say whatever the fuck he thinks, even if we disagree with him.

Ever since 1994 (Gingrich), Republicans have been willing to commit any kind of hypocrisy, break any tradition, smear anyone, lie about anything, bend any rule, exploit any loophole, and generally shrug at any protocol that's an impediment to winning. The Democrats have always been far more concerned about their supposed integrity, which all too often results in not taking clear shots when they have them, not responding in kind to the worst sort of political knee-capping, and generally getting hung up on procedural/traditional points.

Perfect example: during the Bush 43 administration, Republicans were beating them up for filibustering Bush's judicial appointees and threatened "the nuclear option" unless the Dems loosened their chokehold. Instead of daring them to do it, the Dems caved, in exchange for the promise—which was utterly meaningless—that the Republicans would never use the nuclear option themselves and would preserve the Dems' ability to filibuster Supreme Court appointees. Fast-forward ten years, when the Dems really needed to be able to stop the appointment of Gorsuch, which had become possible only because of the GOP's nihilistic refusal to fulfill their responsibilities on Obama's Garland nomination. Of course, the GOP used the nuclear option to make sure its nominee would be confirmed. Anyone who thought the GOP would hold its fire in the name of Senate tradition or fair play is an idiot. The fact that the Democrats insist on playing this game is why they've been losing political power since LBJ. It's Lucy and Charlie Brown and the football. It's also sadism and masochism.

Tag-line for the 1953 movie *One Girl's Confession*: "Maybe I'm bad, but what makes you so good?"

Simon Gray: "But finally no man can speak for the tumult of his time unless he speaks from the tumult of himself"—what Trump either does or pretends to do or does without knowing it or all three (which gives it its immense *frisson*).

While in most people the dominant win/lose American paradigm is tempered by the feeling that really to win one needs also to be good, Trump is simply uninterested in that and believes winning is winning regardless of being good—which comes as a great relief to many people who feel held back by trifling moral concerns.

The White House press conference has long been an exercise in the polite lie or "spin" or distraction, which reporters always knew was a lie, but their role was to pretend to believe it. That's gone now. Much better for a press secretary to say, "Go fuck yourselves," or "We're not telling you."

Or White House state dinners—who gives a shit? Enormous sums are spent so we can pretend for a few hours that we have a royal family and so senators and rich donors can get their balls tickled. A thoroughly useless tradition. Get rid of it.

In other words, what's tragic about Democrats' niceness/ etiquette isn't just that they always lose; it's that it's phony, dishonest, dead. The three-second pause before anything came out of Obama's mouth. Hillary's self-congratulatory smirk when she successfully deployed a euphemism. The addiction to public apology for stupid things that only Anderson Cooper thinks matter at all. This is, more or less, how Washington has been functioning for half a century, and it's an insult to everybody.

Dave Grosby, a Seattle sports-radio talk-show host, is bored beyond belief with his job, but he doesn't do anything with his boredom; he's just bored. Seems to me one has to mask the boredom or make the boredom funny. Something. What Trump does is he shows you how bored he is; he also knows how to *pretend* to act excited; he also shows you the space between the boredom and the excitement; it's a never-ending feedback loop, and the viewer is clued in every second—which feels flattering, fun.

Wilde: "Man is least himself when he talks in his own person. Give a man a mask, and he will show you his true face."

Parker: "For the early punk bands, not being able to play their instruments was a mark of virtue—a blow against the elites, the puffy-haired technocrats with their pointless, 12-minute guitar solos."

"I like how punk pretends to be nihilistic but seems to me to hold out real hope, in the deepest, darkest, most urgent and serious and earnest ways and places," I email my friend Keith Kopka, who writes back:

"I feel exactly the same way about it. In my childhood, punk gave me so much more hope than anything else. It also put me in some strange and dangerous situations with bad people, but I think anything you love blindly can do that.

"Trump has only the destructive side of punk down: the immature, selfish, myopic version. I'm trying to think what band Trump would be if he were a punk band; I see him fitting in nicely with the self-destructive narcissism of GG Allin and The Murder Junkies. In the '90s, record labels were looking to cash in on the success of bands like Green Day and Blink-182 that seem similar to this kind of manufactured rebellion. In the mall, you could buy denim jackets with anarchy patches already sewn onto them. At the time, this bothered me and it still bothers me.

"However, Trump is actually much closer to the Sex Pistols: a band idolized and revered for helping to create the genre. They were messy. They didn't play by the rules. They upset political norms. They're remembered as an authentic entity. And they were 100% fabricated and manicured into existence by Malcolm McClaren, who really just wanted to sell fetish clothing. They were completely manufactured and wildly successful, which allowed them to remain or become willfully unaware of their own fakeness. At least initially, the Pistols didn't really think about the role that McClaren took in packaging the band. They bought their own shtick and just started living it until the shtick was indivisible from their day-to-day lives. At the last Pistols show, Johnny Rotten (either finally getting it or knowing it all along) asked the audience, 'Ever get the feeling you've been cheated?'"

THE WISDOM OF CROWDS, AGAIN.

OCTOBER 19, 2015, FOX NEWS, OFF-AIR—

HANNITY: My daughter plays soccer. The all-county final: They bring in this girl from Ukraine. The other team.

CHRIS CHRISTIE: Right.

HANNITY: And this girl's like 6'1". Total pro. In the country four months. Can't even speak English. I try to talk to her; she doesn't even look at me, looks at the interpreter.

CHRISTIE: Can't speak English?

HANNITY: In the high school four months.

CHRISTIE: A ringer.

HANNITY: They do this so she can go to college.

CHRISTIE: Ah.

HANNITY: And I say to my kid, "Keep trying," and she says, "Do you see her, Dad—hello?"

CHRISTIE: It's rough.

HANNITY: And I can't say anything 'cause then it's, "Sean Hannity's daughter gets special treatment."

CHRISTIE: Four months.

HANNITY: You want to talk about Kerry, Israel?

CHRISTIE: It keeps getting worse.

*

C. J. Polychroniou evokes "a line in which residents are standing, expecting to move forward steadily as they work hard and keep to all the conventional values, but their position in the line has stalled. Ahead of them, they see people leaping forward, but that doesn't cause distress, because it's (allegedly) 'the American way' for merit to be rewarded. What does cause real distress is what's happening behind them. They believe that 'undeserving people' who 'don't follow the rules' are being moved ahead of them by federal government programs they see as designed to benefit African-Americans, immigrants, and others they often regard with contempt."

Mona Chalabi, data editor for the *Guardian*, says, "One poll found that 41 percent of Muslims in [England] support jihad, which is obviously pretty scary, and it was reported everywhere in 2015. When I want to check a number like that, I'll start off by finding the original questionnaire. It turns out that journalists who reported on that statistic ignored a question lower down on the survey that asked respondents how they defined jihad, and most of them defined it as 'Muslims' personal, peaceful struggle to be more religious.' Only 16 percent defined it as 'violent, holy war against unbelievers.' Now, this is the really important point: based on those numbers, it's totally possible that no one in the survey who defined it as 'violent, holy war' also said they support it. Those two groups might not overlap at all. It's also worth asking how the survey was carried out. This was something called an 'opt-in poll,' which means that anyone could have found it on the internet and completed it. There's no way of knowing if those people really even identified as Muslim. And, finally, there were 600 respondents in that poll. There are roughly 3 million Muslims in this country, according to the Pew Research Center. That means the poll spoke to roughly one in every 5,000 Muslims in this country. The survey was conducted by a polling organization called Woman Trend, which was set up by Kellyanne Conway."

YOU DON'T BELIEVE
IN THE GENETIC POOL—
THAT WHAT YOU HAVE
YOU HAVE?

(Trump)

Back to back on NPR on Sunday, on *Radiolab* and *TED Radio Hour*, the host's supposedly cute kid acts as a kind of listener-surrogate, asking his dad about science. Is this a dictum from up high at NPR—no information is interesting unless it's wired first through the cloyingly familial?

Similarly, Brian Williams is unable to discuss any issue whatsoever without immediately personalizing it. To Timothy Snyder, a Holocaust historian and author of *On Tyranny*, Williams says, "My friend's mother is a concentration camp survivor." Some of his best friends are Jewish. "She has a number on her arm." Brian has seen pain up close and personal. "What do you think she's thinking about Charlottesville?" He can connect the dots.

Later, Snyder says, "The threat of totalitarianism has arrived. This is the real thing."

It's not. This is farce. (During the inauguration, I was nearly certain that Andy Kaufman was going to rip off his Trump mask, re-establishing his magnificence.)

"Is the president an autocrat, or does he just play one on TV?"
(*The Economist*)

*

NOVEMBER 17, 2015, FOX NEWS, OFF-AIR—

HANNITY: The news [the Paris bombings] is breaking in your direction.

TRUMP: It's terrible what's happening. You saw the polls? People are scared. They feel safe with me.

*

My physical therapist's intern makes the required compare-and-contrast analogy between Trump condemning NFL players for exercising their First Amendment rights but condoning Charlottesville neo-Nazis for exercising theirs, so I'm a little surprised when, fifteen minutes later, she dismisses, with a pfff and a wave of her hand, "Trump's Jewish lawyers."

Esther Perel's batty theories about fidelity and affairs and marriage and renewal are so charming and popular because they're barely disguised allegories of her parents' survival of Nazi concentration camps and the impossibility of ever getting beyond (especially that) trauma. Perel's marriage advice has next to nothing to do with marriage.

A building in which I teach at the University of Washington is actually named Sieg Hall. How could an academic institution be this tone-deaf as to near-echo? I attempt to petition for a name change, but the request gets lost in the bureaucratic maze, and apparently I don't care enough to pursue it further.

Halfway through the third season of *Fargo*, I was curious whether the parade of anti-Semitism portrayals was purposeful (perhaps related to the East German inquisitor in the opening scene?) or inadvertent. Inadvertent.

*

STERN: Why do you attack Rosie O'Donnell?

TRUMP: When you have bullies, you gotta hit 'em right between the eyes....I understand her. I don't like her. She's not a smart person. She's just a bully—a loudmouth bully....When you're dealing with a vicious person, you have to be vicious....A lot of good friends say, "Donald, why do you attack her?" I say, "Because I have to." Genetically, I have to.

*

JANUARY 2016, FOX NEWS, OFF-AIR—

HANNITY: God, you must be tired.

RAND PAUL: I exercise all the time—train. You must be a black belt by now.

HANNITY: Brown. I take my test in a year. Maybe.

PAUL: Mmm.

HANNITY: You know, I broke my finger.

PAUL: Oh?

HANNITY: Sparring. We weren't supposed to hit in the face.

Guy dropped his head: crack; blood everywhere. It was like a murder scene. Finger is destroyed.

...

HANNITY: God, I hate Colbert. He is such an asshole.

PAUL: I don't think he gets the whole Libertarian thing.

HANNITY: I'm not Libertarian.

PAUL: Right. I know.

HANNITY: Just don't do *The View*.

PAUL: Did *The View*, with Whoopi Goldberg. It was okay.

HANNITY: Last time I was on that, I got into it with Rosie O'Donnell. Fuckin' asshole. Never again, I said.

*

Trump used to refer to Michael Cohen as one of his "sons." Clearly, he prefers Jared Kushner over his own sons. Roy Cohn (*Where's my Roy Cohn?*) and Howard Stern (*We're wackos, right?*) have had an enormous influence upon every aspect of his entire being. In 1991 he said, "And isn't it funny: I've got black accountants at Trump Castle and Trump Plaza. Black guys counting my money! I hate it. The only kind of people I want counting my money are short guys that wear yarmulkes." Fred Trump was arrested at a Klan rally in 1927. Asked if he'd repudiate David Duke, Trump said, "Sure—if it makes you feel better." Speaking to the Republican Jewish Coalition, Trump said, "I'm a negotiator, like you folks; this room negotiates more than any room I've spoken to, maybe more." *I promise you that I'm smarter than Jonathan Leibowitz—I mean Jon Stewart.* Trump is a curious kind of philo/anti-Semite, rather like Henry James being horrified by denizens of the Lower East Side and thereby expressing a baffled and eroticized awe.

I am the least anti-Semitic person you've ever seen.

What Trump learned from Roy Cohn (*a lousy lawyer but a genius*) and Howard Stern: generate attention by being an asshole, cover the universe with mud, court my outrage—

I would like to wish all the fathers, even the haters and losers, a very happy Fathers Day.

Would you like to see Donald Trump on Mt. Rushmore? Yes or No. Reserved for Donald Trump.

Another crucial tactic that Trump learned from Cohn: always and first accuse your enemy of your own sin—*Germany is a captive of Russia.*

I am rubber / You are glue / Whatever you say bounces off me / And sticks to you.

HITLER'S TONE WAS SAID TO BE THE EXACT TONE IN WHICH A GERMAN HUSBAND HARANGUED HIS WIFE.

Robert Mapplethorpe needed Jesse Helms. Andres Serrano needed Rudy Giuliani. Philip Roth needed Irving Hound. Trump needs Elizabeth Warren; her hand-wringing and soprano earnestness could not be the more perfect foil.

According to Anne Carson, "In ancient Greece, high vocal pitch goes together with talkativeness to characterize a person who is deviant from or deficient in the masculine ideal of self-control." And yet listen to how soft Clint Eastwood's voice is— the best possible instrument to express barely repressed rage. As is Trump's voice (whose gossip-girl femininity Anthony Atamanuik captures in his Trump impression on *The President Show*); Trump has virtually no bass.

*

FEBRUARY 6, 2013; STERN: All right, here it is; here's the final question, because I don't want to keep you here all day—

TRUMP: Do you do interviews this long with everybody?

STERN: No, just you; you're good.

TRUMP: I'm the most interesting.

STERN: All right, here it is: You know the game Fuck, Marry, Kill? This is where you have to have sex with one person, you have to marry the other person, but you're gay in this case.

QUIVERS: You're gay?

STERN: Yes. Bill Maher, Barack Obama, and Seth Meyers. You have to kill one, marry one, and have sex with one. What do you do?

TRUMP: Okay. All right. And I'll preface this by saying, unlike Seth Meyers, this is a joke, okay?

STERN: Okay. Go ahead.

TRUMP: Seth Meyers is highly overrated as a comedian, so I think we'll lose him.

STERN: You're gonna kill him?

TRUMP: Yeah. Of the other two, I think I'd probably marry Obama.

STERN: Why?

TRUMP: Because I think he's probably, uh—

STERN: He's in the best shape?

TRUMP: I think he's also a lot smarter than Bill Maher, and I do like intelligence—

STERN: And he's faithful.

TRUMP: I don't know. You tell me—is he faithful?

QUIVERS: Who knows? Who's watching?

TRUMP: Robin, who knows, right? That would be a story, wouldn't it?

STERN: And you would fuck Bill Maher?

TRUMP: Aw geez, I don't know. I don't know.

*

Mira Gonzalez tweets, "Obama probably likes fucking, not 'making love.' That's why he's president." This strikes me as exactly wrong. It's true of Trump.

Lindsey Graham pivots yet again to become one of Trump's most fervent cheerleaders; there's much discussion about Graham doing this in order to try to become Secretary of State when Rex Tillerson resigns. Why does no one mention the likelihood that Trump has threatened to out the just barely closeted Graham? (Is this my awfulness or Trump's?)

The local public radio news reader has what is, to me, an intolerably high-pitched voice. He always sounds anxious and fretful, even (especially) when he's informing us that there may be clouds in the forecast. I want to yell at him (I do yell at him), "Dude, it's weather!"

Why do I find every candidate to replace Robert Siegel, who is retiring from *All Things Considered*, so off-putting? I tell myself that none of their voices—especially Ari Shapiro's—are equal to the moment (they aren't), but it's also just my nostalgia for old-school gravitas.

John Gartner says, "There's something deep in our programming that says, If a homicidal alpha male shows up and he's protecting my group, regardless of what his other faults are, I've got to follow him. That's very primal programming. The demagogues—whether it's someone like Trump or Hitler or Milosevic—manipulate people so that instead of being a German, you're an Aryan; instead of being a Rwandan, you're a Tutsi or Hutu; instead of being a Yugoslav, you're a Serb or Croat. Now it's our gene pool against their gene pool. Trump and his people just made it very explicit. Trump's basic theme is, 'I am the alpha male of the white people. If you want to live, follow me,' and they did."

According to Ivana, Trump kept a book of Hitler's speeches on his bedside table. Asked by Marie Brenner, a *Vanity Fair* reporter, how he came to possess the book, Trump asked her how she came to know this information. She said she didn't remember. Trump claimed that Marty Davis, the former Paramount executive, "gave me a copy of *Mein Kampf*, and he's a Jew." Davis gave him another book, not *Mein Kampf*, and isn't Jewish. Trump, later: "If I had these speeches—and I'm not saying that I do—I would never read them."

Leslie Fiedler once said, "I have, I admit, a low tolerance for detached chronicling and cool analysis. It is, I suppose, partly my own unregenerate nature. I long for the raised voice, the howl of rage or love"—quoted with approval, of course, by *NYT* book critic Dwight Garner. This is aesthetic and moral vanity on both their parts.

I think it matters that Hitler supposedly had a micro-penis and an undescended testicle, that Mao suffered from long periods of impotence. How could it not?

THE AVERAGE MAN'S MIND
IS STRUCTURED FOR FASCISM.

(Wilhelm Reich)

Jason Stanley says, "Trump is an authoritarian who uses speech to define a simple reality that legitimates his value system, leading voters to adopt it. Its strength is that it conveys his power to define reality. Its weakness is that it obviously contradicts it. Denouncing Trump as a liar—or describing him as merely entertaining—misses the point of authoritarian propaganda altogether. Authoritarian propagandists are attempting to convey power by defining reality. The reality they offer is very simple. It's offered with the goal of switching voters' value systems to the authoritarian value system of the leader."

Mussolini described his countrymen as being "a gesticulating, chatterbox, superficial, *carnivalesque* people." Such a great word, in context.

THIS STATEMENT IS FALSE.

Finalizing a deal for a client, Laurie negotiates with a sketchy Russian real estate agent. From the entire populace of *Dead Souls* to Putin himself, such a person is ubiquitous in Russia. Is this type uniquely Russian? I would think not. In any case, I'm Russian on my father's side and identify completely with Muscovite disruption-for-disruption's sake.

My father flew to Providence to attend my college graduation, and the day before the ceremony we went on a tour of the John Brown House at the Rhode Island Historical Society. On and on the docent droned, giving us the official version of American history. My father and I tried not to laugh, but as we went from room to room, we were in an ecstasy of impudent giggles.

According to Adam Curtis, "Vladislav Surkov is one of President Putin's advisors and has helped him maintain his power for fifteen years, but he has done it in a very new way. He came originally from the avant-garde art world, and those who have studied his career say that what Surkov has done is import ideas from conceptual art into the very heart of politics. His aim is to undermine people's perception of the world so they never know what's really happening. Surkov turned Russian politics into a bewildering, constantly changing piece of theater. He sponsored all kinds of groups from neo-Nazi skinheads to liberal human rights groups. He even backed parties that were opposed to President Putin, but Surkov then let it be known that this was what he was doing, which meant no one was sure what was real or fake. As one journalist put it, it's a strategy of power that keeps all opposition constantly confused, a ceaseless shape-shifting that's unstoppable because it's indefinable. Which is exactly what Surkov is alleged to have done in the Ukraine [in 2014].

In typical fashion, as the war began, Surkov published a short story about something he called Non-Linear War, in which you never know what the enemy is really up to, even who they are. The underlying aim, Surkov says, is not to win the war but to use the conflict to create a constant state of destabilized perception in order to manage and control."

Netflix's term for the algorithm it uses to determine what movie you want to watch is "pragmatic chaos."

*

BBC, ON-AIR—

ANN COULTER: For people at allegedly serious networks to be putting out lies about him—I mean, this happened long before Trump, but all the fake rape cases…Ferguson ripped the country apart…the alleged shooting of an unarmed black man…and once Trump came along, it's been through the roof.…The internet is the only place people can get the truth. The idea that bots putting 'likes' on Facebook swung the election is *so* insane, and that's fake news.…The claim that Donald Trump admitted to groping a woman's, you know, "blank" is a lie. He says on the tape—and they edit the tape to lie about it:

"they let you do it"—and they edit that part out of the quote ...
The claim that Trump mocked a disabled man: not only was that
a lie, but the *Washington Post* knew it was a lie because the video
proving that that was a lie they took down from their web page.

LAURIE PENNY: The word-salad that you've just heard come
out of Ann Coulter's mouth is exactly what we're talking about.
What she wants to do is not to make a distinction between what
is true and what is not true; it's just to confuse people and make
it easier for people in power with no scruples to just decide what
is true and what is false.

*

Lesley Stahl, who looks like she's had more work done than
I-90, suddenly remembers that a year and a half ago Trump told
her that he "discredits and demeans the media" so "when you
write negative stories about me, no one will believe you." This is
treated by "the media" as if it were a revelation.

As Trump biographer David Cay Johnston says, "That's the strategy: get bad news out, muddle it, and hope people don't get a
clear appreciation of the facts."

*A prominent businessman who does a lot of business with the Soviet
Union calls to keep me posted on a construction project I'm interested
in undertaking in Moscow. The idea got off the ground after I sat
next to the Soviet Ambassador, Yuri Dubinin, at a luncheon held by
Leonard Lauder, a great businessman who is the son of Estée Lauder.
Dubinin's daughter, it turned out, had read about Trump Tower and
knew all about it. One thing led to another, and now [in 1986] I'm*

talking about building a large luxury hotel, across from the Kremlin, in partnership with the Soviet government. They have asked me to go to Moscow in July.

In January 1987, I got a letter from Dubinin that began, 'It is a pleasure for me to relay some good news from Moscow.' It went on to say that the leading Soviet state agency for international tourism, Goscomintourist, had expressed interest in pursuing a joint venture to construct and manage a hotel in Moscow. On July 4, I flew with Ivana, her assistant Lisa Calandra, and [his longtime personal assistant] Norma [Foederer] to Moscow. It was an extraordinary experience. We toured half a dozen potential sites for a hotel, including several near Red Square. We stayed in Lenin's suite at the National Hotel, and I was impressed with the ambition of the Soviet officials to make a deal.

Adam Davidson: "Trump has expressed many times that he wants a Trump Tower Moscow....Felix Sater starts talking to a guy he grew up with, named Michael Cohen, who became a high-ranking executive at the Trump Organization. Pretty soon, they signed a letter of intent, which is the first phase before a development. But then they're not getting the right permissions from the Russian government, and Michael Cohen sends an email to the PR department at the Kremlin, saying 'Hey, can we get this moving? I represent Donald Trump and we want to make this a deal.' The thing is, this all happens in January 2016, in the middle of the presidential campaign. Trump knew, because Michael Cohen says he spoke to Trump about it three times, that his own high-ranking executive was reaching out to the Kremlin to try and get political favors to get a Trump Moscow built. And I don't know this for sure, but there's certainly a theory that he never imagined he would become president, and the very fact that he authorized this supports that idea."

Pankaj Mishra quotes Thomas Merton—"One day we are going to wake up and find America and Russia in bed together and realize they were married all along"—then says, "What makes Milosz a unique guide to our bewildering age is that he recognized early this marriage made in hell."

Obviously, Putin has an enormous amount of financial and personal *kompromat* on Trump (Don Jr.: "Russians make up a pretty disproportionate cross section of a lot of our assets") and therefore has nearly unlimited leverage over him, but is it not also possibly true that Trump loves being bullied by Putin in the way that Fred Trump bullied him? At the very least, it feels very, very familiar to Trump (still a detective story).

ALL CRITICISM IS
A FORM OF AUTOBIOGRAPHY.

(Wilde)

Fleshler: "As a teenager I lived in Rego Park, from 1967-1970, when Trump was actively managing his dad's rental housing empire in Brooklyn and Queens. We lived on the edge of LeFrak City, a large, middle-class housing development that was, at the time, almost entirely white. The Justice Department sued it for denying apartments to blacks a few years before it sued the Trumpsters for the same thing in 1973.

"The Trump interpretation industry hasn't paid enough attention to the influence on the Donald of aggrieved and frightened white tenants as he was learning his dad's business. That's where he first tuned into and became accountable to The Base we're confronting now. I'm quite sure those tenants and his neighbors in Jamaica Estates—and, of course, his dad—spewed the same kind of casual racism that I heard all the time from my friends' parents, some of whom were lawyers, middle managers, and accountants; they weren't Archie Bunkers. LeFrak City was 'still good'—i.e., there were few blacks. But the middle school that I attended was 'going bad' because it included a lot of black kids from North Corona. The barbarians were always at the gates. It was only a matter of time before they would take over and transform LeFrak into 'Chocolate City.'

"I could hear those white tenants' voices—and their outer-borough inflections—when he made that speech to open his campaign: 'They're bringing crime. They're bringing drugs. They're rapists.'"

Former neighbor of the Trumps: "Trump grew up in white America. White America is a thing of the past....It's the way of the world....The white man's gone."

Ben Maller, who hosts an overnight talk show on Fox Sports Radio, frequently conducts a Procrustean argument against Colin Kaepernick, badly distorting the facts. I listen sometimes to Maller, though, because he 1) has an unbelievably great voice; 2) is funny; and 3) has a tragic view of human existence. The Fox News online feed runs a constant drip of clips about black people misbehaving: a high school teacher seducing her student, a nurse laughing at a WWII vet's request for CPR. Black people are extremely ungrateful for everything white people have done for them. As Trump's election is a not-so-soft assassination of Obama, so, too, is the relentless vilification of Lonzo Ball. It's crucial to white America that this pampered black prince fail. At the end of an article about Charlottesville a reader comments, "It's okay to be white." An African-American journalist says to me, "We're all white supremacists—that's what we've been taught."

The morning after Charlottesville, a young, black woman—a graduate student—and I talk about nothing in particular, not a single syllable of which is not barely coded commentary back to Charlottesville.

Four days after Charlottesville: *Does anyone know I own a house in Charlottesville? It's in Charlottesville. You'll see. It is the winery. I know a lot about Charlottesville. I own one of the largest wineries in the United States, in Charlottesville.*

Three months after Charlottesville, Rita Dove publishes in the *New Yorker* her translation of a Goethe poem: "Above the mountaintops / all is still. Among the treetops you can feel / barely a breath— / birds in the forest, stripped of song. / Just wait: before long / you, too, shall rest." The publication of the poem makes virtually no sense unless the reader knows that Rita Dove is black, lives in Charlottesville, and is married to the German novelist Fred Viebahn. Then it becomes a love poem.

Calling Elizabeth Warren "Pocahontas" at a ceremony honoring Native-American World War II code-talkers, Trump is incapable of leaving a gorgeous moment alone. He always needs to empty it out, flatten it, piss on it (paying Moscow prostitutes to piss on a bed on which Obama slept; visiting a Vegas club called The Act, at which simulated golden showers were the key lure), turn glory or grace to shit, shit on it (instructing Stormy to spank him with an issue of *Forbes* on which he was the cover boy). Whence the origin of the drive? It matters whether it's political calculation (base-building), psychic need (destructiveness as suicide watch), or some combination, and if in combination, in what proportion. The answers aren't clear. I suppose most people don't care what the origins of this are for him, but I do.

"Sexuality is lawless or it is nothing," says Jacqueline Rose, "not least because of its rootedness in our unconscious lives, where all sexual certainties come to grief."

*

TRUMP: Howard is too much like me. I would never allow me to date my daughter.

STERN: We're shallow, right?

TRUMP: We're disgusting people, and I wouldn't allow me to date my daughter, so I wouldn't allow him.

STERN: If Ivanka was dating a black guy, would that freak you out?

TRUMP: Um, you know, of course it wouldn't matter to me.

QUIVERS: Don't look over here.

STERN: What are you looking at Robin for?

TRUMP: Of course, nothing like that would bother me.

STERN: What about Bernie Mac?

TRUMP: It would be a great honor to have Bernie Mac date my daughter. A great, great honor—that is the right answer, right?

*

Is it possible Trump is a fake racist? If so, would that be better or worse than being a real racist?

Re the Central Park Five: *Of course I hate these people, and let's all hate these people because maybe hate is what we need if we're gonna get something done. I want to hate these muggers and murderers. They should be forced to suffer and, when they kill, they should be executed for their crimes.*

Regarding the Orlando shooting: *If some of those wonderful people had guns strapped right here, right to their waist, right to their ankle, and this son-of-a-bitch comes out and starts shooting, and one of the people in the room goes BOOM* [points fingers like guns], *BOOM* [points to head], *you know what? That would have been a beautiful, beautiful sight, folks. That would have been a beautiful, beautiful sight.*

To U.S. soldiers: *I'm financially brave.*

An Xfinity radio commercial informs us that "Speed wins." Wait—what? It's "Speed *kills.*" The ad's elision of the verboten word "kills" make the redacted word resonate that much louder. This is true as well when people say, "…the n-word."

The "shithole" / "shithouse" pseudo-debate actually interests me; "shithouse" you can't see, except, vaguely, as a brick building. "Shithole" you can see—shit coming out of your ass. Trump reportedly said "nigger" in numerous out-takes of *The Apprentice*; when will all the tapes drop? Will no one volunteer to pay off the $10 million penalty for breaking the NDA? What will the consequence be? Will there still be a country? It's the shit itself that disturbs people—the unbearable darkness of blackness.

When Oklahoma State basketball player Marcus Smart was called a "piece of crap" by a Texas Tech fan, Smart interpreted what was said as a "racial epithet" and went into the stands to attack the fan. Chuck Berry was obsessed with shitting on white women and being shat upon by them. The racially closeted Anatole Broyard's shrink told him that he was drawn to blonde women because they're the furthest from the color of shit. Kundera writes that "kitsch is the absolute denial of shit, in both the literal and the figurative senses of the word; kitsch excludes everything from its purview that is essentially unacceptable in human existence."

Jamie Malanowski, *SPY*, 1988: "Barbra Streisand chooses her projects very carefully. It has been three years since her show-offy star turn as a nut in *Nuts*, and only now has she rededicated herself to film, this time as the producer-director-star-despot of *The Prince of Tides*, an adaptation of Pat Conroy's novel that her ex-boyfriend Jon Peters is paying her to make for Columbia Pictures. Streisand's on-the-set demeanor suggests that the *Nuts* magic has yet to wear off. Not too long ago, she chewed out her staff because her trailer was inappropriately equipped. The problem? The motor home's toilet featured an awkwardly placed flush handle that in the cramped trailer required its user to pivot around and risk experiencing a glimpse into the bowl. Under Streisand's maniacal orders, plans were drawn up, at considerable expense, to remount the flushing mechanism so that she would be spared the apparent trauma of turning around. Alas, even this proposed solution failed to satisfy Streisand, who as producer of the film is nominally responsible for keeping the film within budget. She finally decreed that henceforth her underlings find and rent her *houses* near various shooting locations—the main criterion being the grandeur of the houses' bathrooms."

John Kelly says that Dreamers who didn't sign up for DACA are too lazy to get off their asses.

African Americans and Hispanics are living in hell.

Happy #CincoDeMayo! The best taco bowls are made in Trump Tower Grill. I love Hispanics! [photo of Trump eating a taco bowl]

*

OCTOBER 20, 2015, FOX NEWS, OFF-AIR—

HANNITY: He was really on his game today.

PRODUCER: He was great.

HANNITY: [imitating Trump] "Nobody builds a better wall than me. Nobody builds better buildings." Yeah, sure. They'll just crash a plane into the wall and climb over.

*

Dori Monson, "Libertarian" political commentator/Seahawks pre-game and half-time and post-game host: "Really—'Feliz Navidad' as a bump[er]? My least favorite Christmas song ever."

I love "Feliz Navidad." What's not to like?

Monson is making a political point, under the guise of aesthetic judgment.

When my Bread Loaf student Francisco Cantú showed me an early draft of his memoir, *The Line Becomes a River*—about being Latino and a U.S. border guard—I encouraged him to make the manuscript more ambivalent and complicit rather than the easy embodiment of moral outrage. Which he did and which is why, of course, the book is now being attacked.

ProPublica releases a tape of a six-year-old girl crying for her mother and father in a border detention center in Texas. Of course Trump wants to separate children from their parents, destroying the kind of love he never got and can't experience.

Despite all his left-wing bona fides ("I'm a pragmatic European socialist"), Lawrence O'Donnell (Harvard '74), the former Democratic Party political operative and *West Wing* producer who now hosts *The Last Word* on MSNBC, derides Devin Nunes for having attended California Polytechnic/San Luis Obispo; so, too, he mocks Trump for having been outmaneuvered on a particular policy matter by *Mexico*, of all countries. In 2008, during the Democratic primaries, Bill Clinton said to Ted Kennedy about Obama, "Twenty years ago, he would have been carrying our bags."

On a red-eye flight from Seattle to Atlanta, all of the flight attendants are African-American and, without exception, grouchy and/or morose. What a relief. Enough of the pretense.

I have a great relationship with the blacks. It's impossible to overestimate the work done here by the word "the"; again, is he conscious of this, or is it his natural register, or is it his natural register and then is he aware of the value of not veering from that register?

Naipaul: "It was like a chant from her, as we drove [in the American South in the 1980s]. Black people there, black people there, white people there. Black people, black people, white people, black people. All this side black people, all this side white people. White people, white people, black people, white people."

Oh, look at my African-American over there.

*

NOVEMBER 1, 2011; FOX NEWS, ON-AIR—

COULTER: If you are a conservative black, they will believe the most horrible sexualized fantasies of these uptight white feminists.

HANNITY: Why do you think liberals feel so threatened by Herman Cain?

COULTER: Our blacks are so much better than their blacks.

*

Interviewing a candidate for a position on the writing staff of *World News Tonight*, Peter Jennings asked, "How does it feel to be a finalist just because you're black?" The applicant's response: "How does it feel to be on TV just because of your looks?" Needless to say, he got the job.

At the after-party to *Hamilton*'s premiere in Seattle, I learn immeasurably more about politics from people's reactions to the enormous, metal tutu attached to the callipygian African-American dancer's ass than I do during the three-hour play beforehand.

In the American theater of excruciatingly minor reparations, the black character in nearly all shows and movies tends to be an anodyne force for good; so, too, African-American pundits appear increasingly frequently on talk shows, as do biracial couples in commercials.

On *Wait Wait…Don't Tell Me!*, one of the panelists says about Ben Carson, "Well, he would know from stupid." There are a pause and a gasp until the audience realizes the offending party is the screenwriter John Ridley, who's African-American; then everything is okay again.

Josh Harkinson writes that "Richard Spencer envisions a future for the United States along the lines of a 'renewed Roman Empire,' a dictatorship in which the primary criterion for citizenship is whiteness: 'You can't view another white person as your enemy.'… 'Cuckservative,' a term that has recently begun appearing on fringe internet sites, is meant to denigrate mainstream Republicans as impotent traitors—by evoking a porn genre that features white men watching their wives have sex with black men."

*

STERN: Would you date a black woman?

TRUMP: It depends what your definition of "black" is.

*

What I love so much about the video of Bob Dylan singing "Knockin' on Heaven's Door" in Sydney is the song, sure, and the music and the rapport between Dylan and Tom Petty and the audience's reaction and the gorgeous editing, but really it's Dylan's oblique micromanagement of the people on stage, including the black backup singers, The Queens of Rhythm. He's in mortal agony but is in complete command.

Manohla Dargis says, "The greater, graver flaw, the one that empties *Suburbicon* [directed and co-written by George Clooney] out and turns it into a mannerist exercise, is that the movie reproduces the inequality it's ostensibly outraged by. This has less to do with star power and everything to do with emphasis and interest. It's clear, even from her few scenes, including a showdown with a racist, that [Karimah] Westbrook could have made Mrs. Mayers a force if given the chance. Yet despite the parallel editing, despite the scenes of the mob plaguing the Mayerses—and the images of a black mother, father, and son who are sometimes seen but say so little—their terror isn't about them. It's about how bad it makes white people look."

*

AUGUST 2016, MILWAUKEE, MIDDAY, *outside the Pabst Theater, where later in the evening a Fox News Town Hall will feature Hannity, Trump, Sebastian Gorka, Sheriff David Clarke, and several family members of Benghazi victims. Now, a Fox technician has a conversation with Lisa, a local senior citizen and security volunteer; OFF-AIR—*

LISA: I told you it was a beautiful theater.

TECH: You were right.

LISA: I like the concerts best.

TECH: What have you seen that you loved?

LISA: Oh, Heart. Heart came through just a while back. I love Heart.

TECH: "Barracuda."

LISA: I like "Crazy On You."

TECH: What else?

LISA: Lisa Marie Presley was here. She looks just like her dad.

TECH: Sure.

LISA: Some angles, it's spooky.

TECH: The schedule says she's back in September.

LISA: Don't I know it. I'm gonna volunteer to work that show.

TECH: You're a huge fan.

LISA: You bet. She should sing more of her dad's songs, though.

…

Four children, led by two adults, walk by. All the children are under ten—white, middle-class in appearance. The mother is white; the father is black.

...

LISA: Did you see that nigger with them kids?

TECH: [Silence]

LISA: Damnit.

TECH: [Silence]

LISA: Anyway...

TECH: [Silence]

LISA: "Suspicious Minds."

TECH: [Silence]

LISA: That's the song I like: "Suspicious Minds."

APOCALYPSE ALWAYS

WE'RE WORSE THAN LIONS.
AT LEAST THEY DO IT FOR FOOD.
WE DO IT FOR THE THRILL
OF THE HUNT.

(Trump)

Jane Lynch says about her *Glee* character, Sue Sylvester, "No one is that cocksure unless she's hiding something."

When still at Fox, Megyn Kelly, to herself, off-air: "I'm gonna be so good. So good….I'm not ready."

Jon Gruden, the newly hired coach of the Oakland Raiders, is said to possess something called "a big personality"; what this actually means, at ground level, is that he's a bullshit artist (Obama's exact term for Trump).

D. H. Lawrence: "Men can suck the heady juice of exalted self-importance from the bitter weed of failure."

Antonio Porchia: "Man is weak, and when he makes strength his profession, he is weaker."

Our cat, Zoomer, was exceedingly centripetal and social. The moment I spread out my papers on the dining room table, he would lie on top of them. He greeted most visitors by crawling onto their laps. His favorite activity was lying in front of the fire for hours while Laurie, Natalie, and I sat near him, reading. His second favorite activity was to lie between the three of us while we were watching a movie; he ate ice cream from our bowls while we pretended not to notice. At night, he slept in the crook of Laurie's neck, his paws wrapped around her forehead. And yet if we indulged him by petting him for too long, he inevitably reacted to this overdomestication by biting or scratching us. He loved to hide behind a bookcase and swat unsuspecting passersby or lie across the bookcase, one paw hanging in the air, and look out across the room—a lion surveying the savannah, scoping antelope. He wanted to convince himself and us that, thoroughly pampered though he was, at heart he was a killer.

From room to room he dragged "his" teddy bear—what Natalie called his girlfriend—and, despite his supposedly having been fixed years before, dry-humped it day and night, howling with a conqueror's fury. He'd spend hours scratching the window at his neighborhood nemesis, Fireball, but when presented with the opportunity to confront Fireball nose-to-nose, he always settled, pseudo-disappointedly, for the safety of imprisonment. On the rare occasions when he did go outside, he hissed, terrified, at all provocations and scooted inside on the flimsiest pretext. He needed to convince himself that he was a tough guy, but really Zoomy was a pussy.

HEROES.

A middle-aged woman is standing too close to me at the ATM. I ask her to step back.

She refuses, saying, "Do I make you nervous?"

"Yes, exactly. You make me nervous."

"I'm not looking at your PIN."

"I don't care." We're at a bit of an impasse. I double-down on my own craziness. "Please stand back."

The coffee-shop owner down the street is fanatically antipathetic to all things Trump, but in the obsessiveness with which he places innumerable signs throughout the shop informing customers what they can and can't do and when they can and can't do it, he could not be more Trumpian.

Can one say, coherently, that one is a truly tolerant person if one refuses to tolerate intolerance? A tricky problem in logic, but there may be much riding on our ability to resolve it.

In the hot tub with his five-year-old son and gorgeous wife, the father is all lovey-dovey with his son. In the locker room, the father is a complete asshole to the little guy.

Christine Quinn, the first female and openly gay Speaker of the NYC City Council, is on MSNBC, talking about the 2017 terrorist attack that killed eight people near the World Trade Center. According to Quinn, New York is the greatest city in the world; 9/11 was the worst terror attack in the history of the world; New Yorkers have the greatest will of any people in the world; etc.; etc. She's Trump.

Forced by circumstance to reread my first novel, *Heroes*, which was published almost thirty-five years ago, I'm dismayed to be reminded that my protagonist, a sportswriter in the upper Midwest, chooses, as if in pre-echo of the 2016 election, to reify a self-healing mythology rather than confront messy and harmful truths.

Michael Moore says, "Minnesota once elected a professional wrestler as its governor. Voters didn't do this because they were stupid or thought that Jesse Ventura was some sort of statesman. They did it just because they could….[In 2015] Elmer Gantry shows up, looking like Boris Johnson [Moore wants to make sure that you know he knows who Elmer Gantry and Boris Johnson are] and just saying whatever shit [this is Moore reminding you he's from Flint] he can make up to convince the masses that this is their chance to stick it to all of them who have wrecked their American Dream. The Outsider has arrived to clean house [this is Moore reminding you that his own brand is still, sort of, The Outsider]. You don't have to agree with him. You don't even have to like him. He's your personal Molotov cocktail to throw right into the center of the bastards who did this to you [could not be more Trumpian in its rhetoric]. Send a message. Trump is your messenger."

In a cartoon called "Aspirational Trump Tower," two schlubs (husband-and-wife tourists) take a double selfie outside Trump Tower. The cartoonist feels compelled to add, "This will give you a better understanding of Trump's base than 1,000 of those 'What do Trump supporters think?' essays." Astonishingly, the cartoonist doesn't get how Trumpian this self-congratulation-via-putdown is.

Adrian Wooldridge, an editor of the *Economist*, says, "A Manhattan-based playboy who has had life handed to him on a silver platter might look like a strange vehicle for the pain of the heartland, but Trump is a winner with the soul of a loser. He is consumed by imagined slights to his fragile ego, hypersensitive to the pretensions of smarty-pants liberals, a man who spends many hours a day watching cable news and seething with anger."

Schwartz: "From the very first time I interviewed him in his office in Trump Tower in 1985, the image I had of Trump was that of a black hole. Whatever goes in quickly disappears without a trace. Nothing sustains. It's forever uncertain when someone or something will throw Trump off his precarious perch—when his sense of equilibrium will be threatened and he'll feel an overwhelming compulsion to restore it. Beneath his bluff exterior, I've always sensed a hurt, incredibly vulnerable little boy who just wanted to be loved. What Trump craves most deeply is the adulation he has found so fleeting."

I love losers because they make me feel so good about myself.

We invent idols that contain the contradictions within ourselves. Ichiro, Madonna, Elvis, and Jesus, for example, are all somehow—simultaneously, impossibly—avatars of both absolute conformity and absolute rebellion.

The Caroline Kennedy Foundation is going to announce its "Profile in Courage" winner any day now, and Brian Williams announces that he's obsessed each year with trying to figure out who's going to receive the award, precisely because he has boyish fantasies of one year being named the winner of the award (back to pretending he was taking incoming when on that brief journalistic jaunt through Iraq) but could not be more obsequious to his guests.

For a week I'm staying at the same hotel in Moscow, Idaho, where the Idaho Juvenile Justice Association conference is being held. A muscular counselor wears a T-shirt that says OBAMA CAN'T TAKE AWAY THESE GUNS. I go out of my way to be especially friendly to the flipper-handed hotel clerk, but when my cab needs to leave for the airport and she can't find my credit card, I fly into a brief and very Trumpian fit.

The January 2018 issue of the *Brown Alumni Magazine* quotes Glenn Kessler ('81), who writes the "Fact Checker" column in the *Washington Post*: "Man has been spreading fake news since he learned to talk." In the same issue, Lily Cohen ('11)'s quite brilliant "Class Note" reads, "I am pleased to announce that I will be moving to the Hamptons, where I designed a modest mansion, which was inspired by Kim Kardashian's re-imagining of Jackie O.

I am excited that Snuffles, my small corgi, will have more space to run and play. You can contact me @lilyofthepingo."

My friend Robert, a playwright who's a building super in Queens, says, "I've noticed that all of people's daily unhappiness and existential terror gets projected onto their perceived apartment woes. Most tenants come home unconsciously stewing from their pent-up rage and despair from having to suck up to their bosses. On top of that, they're flooded with anxiety and impotent rage at the horror-show that is the falling apart of humanity under late-stage capitalism (and Trump), compounded by the internet, Facebook, Twitter, etc.—which shoves all the hatred, illness, and poverty of the universe in their faces, with occasional videos of cute animals punctuating the horror.

"They're barely holding it together when they come home, eager to dissociate as much as possible from reality, and then suddenly, as they're about to swoon off into a beautifully dissociative coma, they hear the tenant upstairs walking across the floor WITHOUT A CARPET and WITHOUT TAKING OFF THEIR FUCKING SHOES GODDAMNIT AND PLAYING THEIR MUSIC TOO LOUD, and they have a massive fit and call me to tell me that the people above them are DISTURBING THEM during the one moment when they want to just drink or get high or basically tune out the universe, which includes the REAL ISSUE that people are running from, which is that no matter what they do, how much money they make, how much sex they have, or how much they suck up to the universe, they know in their bones that they are EVENTUALLY GOING TO GET SICK AND DIE.

"I had one tenant, the president of the condo board, buzz me after a massive snowstorm and insist that I remove all the snow so the roof wouldn't collapse. When I explained to him that there was nowhere to put all the roof snow, he threatened to have me fired. (Later, he sent a letter to the board of directors, claiming that the stonemason who had done the work on his fireplace had chiseled secret pornographic images into the stones, and he demanded that they be removed at once; he even sent photos with captions like 'Here is a photo of two people doing it doggie-style'—which he had helpfully circled in the photo. So he may not be a representative example of my 'average' tenant.) Most of the time I listen and nod and allow them to discharge their frustrations and, after several minutes of my agreeing and consoling, they seem to feel a little less upset.

"Shortly after 9/11, one tenant called me and, his voice quivering with rage, told me that someone had rung his apartment doorbell and, when he asked who it was, the answer was, 'The exterminator.' The tenant wanted me to know that that REALLY, REALLY upset him, and he wanted it to NEVER, EVER HAPPEN AGAIN. As it turned out, it actually was the exterminator who was checking to see if he had a mouse or bug issue. Then there was the time someone buzzed me in the middle of the night. When I opened the door, I saw my first-floor tenant lying on the carpet in pain with her hand jammed into a large fax machine. Apparently, she had tried to remove a piece of paper and got her hand stuck inside the machine; in a panic, she had carried it up three flights of stairs and lay on the ground until I could liberate her. When I freed her hand, she left immediately, never spoke to me again, and moved out the next week."

HALLELUJAH.

Reading Robert Hass's "A Poem," about the atrocity of aerial bombardment, I perk up only when I notice his clear misspelling—"principle" for "principal." This is a kind of fascism on my part.

My Uber driver, a veteran, seems pretty chill until he asks me what my most recent book, *War Is Beautiful*, is about, and when I say to him that it's a critique of how *NYT* front-page photographs beautified and glamorized the Afghanistan and Iraqi wars, his right arm jounces uncontrollably and doesn't stop even when we arrive at the airport.

Kinda giddy when Brian Williams, drunk on U.S. missile strikes in Syria, quotes (without comprehending even slightly) Leonard Cohen's line "I'm guided by the beauty of our weapons," then says about bombing vids, "They are beautiful pictures." For a day or two, Instagram "blows up" with *War Is Beautiful* photos.

When I visit a photography course to discuss this book, a beautiful, blonde, seemingly bored woman sits quietly throughout the conversation until the professor, echoing Franz Kafka's well-rubbed formulation, claims that my book is an attempt to "break the frozen sea within us." She erupts, saying, "Nothing can break through. We're numb. There's no going back. No image, no matter how horrifying, can touch us." It's the first time I've felt anything in a very long time.

REGENERATION
THROUGH VIOLENCE.

(Richard Slotkin)

My writer-friend Joni Tevis rhapsodizes to me about *Twister*, which she agrees is a terrible movie but which she loves: "Something in me, in us, wants destruction (our mortality) to catch up with us at last. Everything we do to try to fend off the category-5 tornado must finally fail—'incredible phenomena will occur'—and if we survive something like that, we just have to be lucky, and sooner or later we won't be. So instead of throwing up these frail barks of defense (the sad little motor court and Quonset hut that get flattened at the end of the movie), eventually we/I just want to welcome this thing we've been running to or from and get a good look at it and do what we can against it, which isn't much. Something in it makes me want it to come."

At first, I misread what Joni had written as "makes me want to come."

CNN headline: "Joel Taylor of *Storm Chasers* Dead at 38."

Joni: "Does Trump's base crave destruction, crave some kind of fellow-feeling—that at least now the rest of the world, the elites, are feeling some of the same despair that they've been feeling for generations? I don't think so."

Oh, I do.

I say to Joni that the essence of *The Shining* is, "Here we are in perfect paradise. Let's make sure we create hell on earth." She says "No, it's, 'We carry our hell wherever we go.'"

Campbell McGrath says, "'To each according to his needs and from each according to his abilities' is a beautiful precept but not realistic in regard to actual human beings, who are violent ape creatures let loose on the planet with a will to destroy everything they can get their hands on. That's us."

Some sort of bogus Emergency Expert shows up on NPR to claim that when we're watching disaster coverage (Texas and Florida hurricanes), we're doing so out of compassion/concern for our fellow citizens. This is utterly wrong. We watch to feel safe, wrapped in a cocoon of voyeurism and vicariousness and Schadenfreude. We like to see bad things happen to other people. This is terrible, but it's true. The clown Avner the Eccentric can easily walk straight between two trees on a slack rope, but for his act he wavers back and forth, mocks alarm, all but falls, and just makes it across. People dearly want him to fall. We will do anything to disrupt our lives. We worship chaos. It's impossible not to rubberneck.

According to D. H. Lawrence, the mind hates knowing that it's engaged in violence, but in reality people actually enjoy it.

Apparently, it's pleasurable—even "orgasmic"—for us to participate in bloodshed but remain unconscious of our role in it.

My grandniece, a third-grader in Brooklyn Heights, explaining the insidious appeal of the class bully: "He's awful—everyone hates him—but he makes things more interesting."

Nathanael West writes, "Once there [in California], they [Midwest transplants now living in LA] discover that sunshine isn't enough. They get tired of oranges, even of avocado pears and passion fruit. Nothing happens. They don't know what to do with their time. They haven't the mental equipment for leisure, the money, nor the physical equipment for pleasure. Did they slave so long just to go to an occasional Iowa picnic? What else is there? They watch the waves come in at Venice. There wasn't any ocean where most of them came from, but after you've seen one wave, you've seen them all. The same is true of the airplanes at Glendale. If only a plane would crash once in a while so that they could watch the passengers consumed in a 'holocaust of flame,' as the newspapers put it. But the planes never crash."

A junior high kid in the pool locker room sings Randy Rainbow's parody of Luis Fonsi's "Despacito"—"Desperate Cheeto," about Trump: "How can we have chosen such a mental case? / Every day you devastate the human race. / ... And will our country still be here / At the end of your four years?" None of the kid's friends can stop laughing, but from up under the floorboards you can feel (I feel I can feel) the kids quaking in their flip-flops.

Harry Connick Jr. and his wife, Jill Goodacre, appear on the cover of *People* magazine because she has breast cancer. *People* chooses a picture that emphasizes how large her breasts once were (or how large her reconstructed breasts are?). The point of this is for us to root against Harry and Jill. We pretend to be empathetic, but what we want is for the beautiful people to fail and fall.

Guy falls from a 50-story building; as he flies by the 25th floor, someone asks him how it's going. Guy says, "So far, so good."

In his essay "Apocalypse Always," Walter Kirn empties out the mawkishness of nearly every pseudo-dystopian novel, in which the narrator always turns out to be humanity's last chance. In reality, there's no such person left.

Amis is writing a "novel" about Christopher Hitchens, Saul Bellow, and Philip Larkin; in every interview Amis has ever given, he says that the novel, as a form, is the last vehicle left for something called "freedom," but the only reason anyone would read his book is for the gossip.

Here's the Statue of Liberty—one of the truly beautiful symbols of anything anywhere in the world.

When I ask a Jeb Bush policy advisor to tell me stories about what it was like to be part of a presidential campaign, she tells me half a dozen anecdotes, each of which is a sort of earnest ode to the integrity, thoughtfulness, and idealism of the candidate. I literally can't comprehend how someone can think about other people this way. It's the same thing that made *The West Wing* nearly impossible for me to watch. I think we are a fallen, doomed species.

Renata Adler writes, "We were talking about *No, No, Nanette*. I said I thought there was such a thing as an Angry Bravo—that those audiences who stand, and cheer, and roar, and seem altogether beside themselves at what they would instantly agree is at best an unimportant thing, are not really cheering *No, No, Nanette*. They are booing *Hair*. Or whatever else it is on stage that they hate and that seems to triumph. So they stand and roar. Every bravo is not so much a Yes to the frail occasion they have come to make a stand at, as a No, goddam it to everything else, a bravo of rage. And with that, they become, for what it's worth, a constituency that is political. When they find each other, and stand and roar like that, they want, they want to be reckoned with." Why does Adler repeat "they want"? She is showing you the power of song.

Adler emails me, "I think these are the end times. I guess I have thought that before, but that was probably at the beginning of the end times. This seems like the end of the end. It really feels like the end of the world."

I pretend to agree but actually don't. Stalingrad will hold (just barely). Wrong metaphor, but here's why—

PEOPLE LIKE A HERO, A GOLDEN BOY, BUT MANY LIKE A FALLEN HERO EVEN BETTER.

(Trump)

What's great about Scorsese's remake of *Cape Fear* is what makes Flannery O'Connor's "A Good Man Is Hard to Find" great: the homicidal Misfit is nothing more or less than the logical extension of the venality of everyone else in the narrative. (Look again at both titles.)

Everyone's ambition is underwritten by a tragic flaw. We're deeply divided animals who are drawn to the creation of our own demise. Freud says, "What lives wants to die again. The life-drive is in them, but the death-drive as well." (Notice that he says "them.") Kundera writes, "Anyone whose goal is 'something higher' must expect someday to suffer vertigo. What is vertigo— fear of falling? No, vertigo is something other than fear of falling. It's the voice of the emptiness below us that tempts and lures us; it's the desire to fall, against which, terrified, we defend ourselves." And the more righteous our self-presentation, the more deeply we yearn to transgress, to fall, to fail—because being bad is more interesting, exciting, and erotic than being good. Eliot Spitzer had to demolish the perfect marble statue he'd made of himself: the image of perfect rectitude (the converse, of course, is Trump craving the Peace Prize). We all contrive different, wonderfully idiosyncratic, and revealing ways to remain blind to our own blindnesses.

Richard Nixon had to undo himself, because—as hard as he worked to get there—he didn't believe he belonged there. Bill Clinton's fatal charm was/is his charming fatality: his magnetism is his doom; they're the same trait. Someone recently said to me about Clinton, "He could have been, should have been, one of the great presidents of the twentieth century, so it's such a shame that—" No. No. No. There's no "if only" in human nature. When Bush 43 was a young man, he asked his father, "You want to go *mano a mano* right here?" The war of terror was the not-so-indirect result. In short, what animates us inevitably ails us.

When my difficult heroes (and all real heroes are difficult) self-destruct, I retreat and reassure myself that it's safer here close to shore, where I live. I distance myself from the disaster, but I gawk in glee (I want the good in my heroes, the gift in them, not the nastiness, or so I pretend). Publicly, I tsk-tsk, chastising their transgressions. Secretly, I thrill to their violations, their (psychic or physical) violence, because through them I vicariously renew my acquaintance with my shadow side. By detaching, though, before free fall, I reserve my distance from death, staving off difficult knowledge about the exact ratio in myself of angel to animal.

According to A. C. Bradley, "No play at the end of which the hero remains alive is, in the full Shakespearean sense, a tragedy. On the other hand, the story depicts also the troubled part of the hero's life which precedes and leads up to his death, and an instantaneous death occurring by 'accident' in the midst of prosperity would not suffice for it. It is, in fact, essentially a tale of suffering and calamity conducting to death. The suffering and calamity are, moreover, exceptional. They befall a conspicuous person. They are themselves of some striking kind. They are also, as a rule, unexpected, and contrasted with previous happiness or glory. A tale, for example, of a man slowly worn to death by disease, poverty, little cares, sordid vices, petty persecutions, however piteous or dreadful it might be, would not be tragic in the Shakespearean sense. Such exceptional suffering and calamity, then, affecting the hero, and—we must now add—generally extending far and wide beyond him, so as to make the whole scene a scene of woe, are an essential ingredient in tragedy and a chief source of the tragic emotions and especially of pity. But the proportions of this ingredient, and the direction taken by tragic pity, will naturally vary greatly. Pity, for example, has a much larger part in *King Lear* than in *Macbeth* and is directed in the one case chiefly to the hero, in the other chiefly to minor characters."

Bosley Crowther's *NYT* review in 1956 of Sir Laurence Olivier's *Richard III*: "For Richard, the dark, misshapen monster of the English House of York in those medieval years when it was waging the War of the Roses with the stubborn Lancasters, is the towering focal figure in this complex drama of plots and murders at court. Sir Laurence's Richard is a weird, poisonous portrait of a super-rogue whose dark designs are candidly acknowledged with lick-lip relish and sardonic wit....He has an electric vitality and a fascinatingly grotesque grace. A grating voice, too, is a feature of his physical oddity....

"From a glib and egotistical conniver at the outset of the play, when he confides his clever purpose to the audience and hypocritically woos Lady Anne, he becomes a cold and desperate tyrant after he has ordered Clarence and Hastings dispatched and faces up to the horror of slaying the little princes in the Tower. And then, toward the end, he is lost of all feeling save terror and a horrible dread of his date. Sir Laurence, as director as well as actor, has clearly and artfully contrived to emphasize Richard's isolation and his almost pathetic loneliness....

"No wonder one feels some sorrow for him—for this dark gangster of another age—when he dies on the ground, thrashing in torment, with spears sticking in him like a pig."

Peace: the universal yearning of every human soul. If there's one thing that Trump disbelieves, it's this. He's much more closely attuned to what Hawkes once called "the terrifying similarity between the unconscious desires of the solitary man and the disruptive needs of the visible world." Or, as Elizabeth Bowen writes about the protagonist of her novel *The Heat of the Day* (set in London during the blitz and published in 1948), "She could no more blame the world than one can blame any fellow sufferer: in these last twenty of its and her own years, she had to watch in it what she felt in herself—a clear-sightedly helpless progress toward disaster. The fateful course of her fatalistic century seemed more and more her own."

I'm very much a fatalist. I always have been, but I'm more so now.

Harold Brodkey quotes Neal Gabler on Walter Winchell: "All that would remain was this image of an angry, mean, foolish old man railing at the fates that had betrayed him." This is journalism and is boring. Brodkey then pivots and says, "He railed at fate, he fought it, and he won for a while—and, of course, he lost in the end. And it broke him. It is practically everyone's story." This is tragedy and is beautiful.

I loved Orson Welles. He was totally fucked up. He was a total mess. But think of his wives. Think of his hits. He was like this great genius that, after twenty-six, never did it. He thought everybody was a moron. Everybody was this. Everybody was that. If he had a budget, he'd exceed it by twenty times and destroy everything. He became totally impossible. I loved that.

BLACK PLANET.

Trump is always playing Trump—fighting to win, but win what or why? He has no clue and knows he has no clue. And we know he has no clue. And he knows we know he has no clue. And his lostness, his irreducible sadness, is what I find so compelling, almost moving, about him.

Trying (failing) to adapt my book *Black Planet: Facing Race during an NBA Season* into a documentary film, the director says to me, "I think there's something a little bit scary about you. I like you a lot, but when I come close to you, I feel this desire on your part to just go after everything, including the things that both you and I love, and there are certain things that I don't want to destroy."

Roger Stone says that Trump testifying before Mueller would be a "suicide mission," a "death wish." Stone doesn't get, or pretends not to get, how exhilarated and liberated Trump is by this moment of undoing. He's been building toward this moment his whole life. It's very deep in him.

He hates himself, which is why he always projects onto his opponents all of his own sins. How crazy is the Trumpian projection? Part of the gas-lighting is that you can't tell.

A bully to me is someone who is trying to work out some psychological problem by intimidating others.

Wait—what?

Robert Ripley was curious in both senses: first, his life was un-believable to himself; and second, he couldn't feel life as a real thing, so he endlessly collected unbelievable bits of ephemera to make clear to himself that the world was as strange as he was, and also that he was equal to the world. Ripley helped to create the world in which we now live.

Country music is always and forever about one thing: shit happens. Trump is the most obvious country song ever written: the more braggadocious the utterance, the more emphatically it reveals his level of distress, anxiety, and ennui.

BLEEDING OUT.

Trump is obsessed with death and has no access to any sort of spiritual feeling or even yearning. I'd be shocked if he hasn't arranged to have himself cryogenically frozen.

*

QUIVERS: How do you feel about being a grandfather?

TRUMP: Not good.

QUIVERS: You don't let them call you "Grandpa"?

TRUMP: No, I don't. And I don't consider myself a grandfather. I don't even want to hear the term.... There's nothing good about the clock.

*

Whence the origin of the popularity of the term "bleed out"— *ER?* Why do so many people love to say it now? The phrase makes life seem serious—these bodies we're carrying around: ultimately, they all just stop—which Trump is even more obsessed with than most humans are.

At Mar-a-Lago, we had this incredible Red Cross ball. All these rich people are there to celebrate the Marines, but they're really there to get their picture in the Palm Beach Post. *They're giving me $100,000 a table, and they don't even know where the money's going; they could care less. A man, about 80 years old—very wealthy; a lot of people didn't like him—fell off the stage. This guy falls on his face, hits his head, and I thought he died. You know what I did? I said, 'Oh my god, that's disgusting,' and turned away. I couldn't—he was right in front of me and I turned away. I didn't want to touch him. He was bleeding all over the place. Marble floors—didn't look so good. They changed color.*

I've never been terribly interested in what people give [to charity]*, because their motivation is rarely what it seems to be, and it's almost never pure altruism.*

Kafka: "Miserliness is, after all, one of the most reliable signs of profound unhappiness. Nothing alive can be calculated."

What a scene. It was a blast. You see, I can have fun, too. It's all part of the formula.

*

QUIVERS: Are you a happy man, Donald?

TRUMP: Uh, yes, I think so. I mean, I like to say I'm a content man. I don't know if I'm capable of happiness, okay?

WE HAVE MET THE ENEMY
AND HE IS US.

I've been a good father—really good—but I've never been that in-volved. Like, if they ever said, "Come on, Dad, let's have a catch in Central Park," I'd say, "Excuse me?"

Trump once described someone (probably Andrew Stein, former Manhattan Borough president) "being hit over the head with a cannon." Trump is, to me, a bit like certain ath-letes, if one can say that, or other people who speak in entirely demotic language; it's never quite clear whether he's illiterate ("North Korea best not"; "very epic"; "very stable genius"; apropos structuring a season of *The Apprentice* around the opposition of a white team against a black team: "Whether people like that idea or not, it is somewhat reflective of our very vicious world") or whether his malapropisms are (at least occasionally) an intentional form of modest witticism and/or faux-populism, the key test-case being, "I'm, like, a really smart person." The "like" here is Ashbery-level genius.

I know him [Bill Belichick], *like, well.*

I've known Paris Hilton from the time she was 12.…She's incredibly beautiful…dumb like a fox."

One of the unique ways in which Trump talks is that he always listens to himself talking and is in active, perpetual, tragicomic dialogue/debate with what he's just said—his inability, in other words, to believe anything. (Montaigne: "We are, I know not how, double within ourselves, with the result that we do not believe what we believe and we cannot rid ourselves of what we condemn.") In a sense, Trump has the tendencies of a (very bad) personal essayist. Told that he can't say X and do Y, he must say X and do Y; so, too, he has an Updikean need to articulate every thought he has ever had—

I'm very well behaved, actually. Almost always. I'm very down the middle.

The truth is, I think the most interesting aspect of that book [The Art of The Comeback] is the loyalty area—the loyalty chapter; I think it's really good. I don't know why I'm promoting a book that's not going to come out for three or four months.

I love all people, rich or poor, but in those particular positions I just don't want a poor person. Does that make sense? Does that make sense? If you insist, I'll do it, but I like it better this way. Right?

I don't think they're that far off. I don't think we're that far, after last week. Famous last words, right? I think we'll get there.

Asked to describe his "brand," Trump says (listen to the declension), "A luxury brand....It's a very successful brand and it does well....I think it's a brand where people know we get things done."

The most interesting thing about him to me, by far, is his commitment to self-immolation, which is unmissable and unending.

The message now is, 'It's a fix.' I've been able to message it.

The performer is always melancholy.

Fame is attention and attention is love and love can convert into hatred in an instant, because it's impossible to get enough love.

James Comey: "This president does not reflect the values of this country."

Ford Madox Ford: "We are all so afraid, we are all so alone, we all so need from the outside the assurance of our own worthiness to exist."

Pogo: "We have met the enemy and he is us."

CITATIONS
Numbers refer to pages in this book:

EPIGRAPH

9 **Adam Curtis**, *Hypernormalisation*
https://www.bbc.co.uk/programmes/p04b183c

A RAGE TO INJURE WHAT'S INJURED US

13 **Jane Wong**, fragment from "Nothing Else!"
https://www.arkint.org/issue-three/
Nicanor Parra, "Sorry to Be So Blunt, General"
https://twitter.com/openpoetrybooks/status/843566866215796736
The Michael Medved Show, author's transcription

14 **Donald Trump**, *The Apprentice*, season 5, episode 12
Noam Chomsky, interviewed by Deborah Solomon, "The
Professorial Provocateur," *The New York Times*, November 2, 2003
https://chomsky.info/20031102/
Trump with Tony Schwartz, *The Art of the Deal*
https://youtu.be/aeQOJZ-QzBk

16 **Trump**, *The Howard Stern Show*, October 10, 2006
Trump, *The Howard Stern Show*, February 6, 2013
Trump, *The Howard Stern Show*, October 10, 2007

17 **Naomi Watts**, *Gypsy*, season 1, episode 10

19 **Trump**, "Special Report: Why Trump Won," *CNN*, November 26, 2017
http://transcripts.cnn.com/TRANSCRIPTS/1711/26/csr.01.html

20 **Tristan Harris**, "How Technology is Hijacking Your
Mind—from a Magician and Google Design Ethicist," *Medium*,
May 18, 2016
https://medium.com/thrive-global/how-technology-hijacks-peoples-minds-from-a-magician-and-google-s-design-ethicist-56d62ef5edf3
David Frum, quoted in Isaac Chotiner, "David Frum Is Still a
Republican. But…," *Slate*, January 22, 2018
https://slate.com/news-and-politics/2018/01/david-frum-on-how-trumpism-has-changed-him.html

Jonathan Martin, Instagram post, February 23, 2018
https://me.me/i/imart-16m-jamesdunleavy-tjtaylr-68incognito-mikepouncey-when-youre-a-bully-20741870

21 **Francis Wilkinson**, "Trump's massive but paper-thin ego will make it difficult to improve for the next debate," *National Post*, September 29, 2016
https://nationalpost.com/opinion/francis-wilkinson-trumps-massive-but-paper-thin-ego-will-make-it-difficult-to-improve-for-the-next-debate
Trump, Stormy Daniels's discussion of Trump in *InTouch*, May 2011
https://www.intouchweekly.com/posts/stormy-daniels-full-interview-151788
Trump's childhood friend, quoted in Michael Kruse, "The Mystery of Mary Trump," *Politico*, November/December 2017
http://politi.co/2zgb99o

22 **Pema Chödrön**, *Practicing Peace in Times of War*

24 **Trump**, *The Howard Stern Show*, April 12, 2010
Trump, *The Howard Stern Show*, February 6, 2013
Trump, *The Howard Stern Show*, February 6, 2013
Tim O'Brien, *Dirty Money*, season 1, episode 6

25 **Trump**, phone conversation reported in Howard Kurtz, *Media Madness*
Trump with Schwartz, *The Art of the Deal*
Fred III, in David Cay Johnston, *The Making of Donald Trump*
Trump, *The Apprentice*, season 11, episode 10
Trump with Schwartz, *The Art of the Deal*

26 **Trump**, on Gary Cohn, in Tim Haines, "Trump: 'Everybody Wants to Work in the White House,'" *Real Clear Politics*, March 6, 2018
https://www.realclearpolitics.com/video/2018/03/06/trump_everybody_wants_to_work_in_the_white_house.html
Off-air conversation between Sean Hannity and Donald Rumsfeld, anonymous Fox News source
Trump, *The Apprentice*, season 7, episode 5

27 **Trump**, *The Howard Stern Show*, January 13, 1997
Trump with Schwartz, *The Art of the Deal*
Trump, on his first State of the Union address, January 30, 2018
https://www.pbs.org/newshour/politics/
trump-says-it-will-be-hard-to-unify-country-without-a-major-event
Trump with Schwartz, *The Art of the Deal*

28 **Trump** with Kate Bohner, *The Art of the Comeback*
Dorothy Dinnerstein, *The Mermaid and the Minotaur*

29 **Trump**, quoted in Corey Lewandowski, *Let Trump Be Trump*
Peter Lovenheim, "Donald Trump's Mommy Issues," *Politico*,
May 13, 2018
https://politi.co/2IdxWbt

30 **Maryanne Trump**, Trump's eldest sister, on Fred Trump, quoted
in Kruse, "The Mystery of Mary Trump," *Politico*, November/
December 2017
http://politi.co/2zgb99o
Selina Scott, "The comb-over creep who hates women—and I
should know," *Daily Mail*, January 30, 2016
http://www.dailymail.co.uk/news/article-3424519/The-comb-creep-hates-
women-know-SELINA-SCOTT-reveals-Donald-Trump-failed-seduce-stalked-
20-years.html
Childhood friend on Mary Trump, quoted in Kruse, "The
Mystery of Mary Trump," *Politico*, November/December 2017
http://politi.co/2zgb99o
Trump, quoted in Aris Folley, "Ian Bremmer: Trump tossed candy to
Merkel at G-7, said 'don't say I never give you anything,'" *The Hill*, June
20, 2018
http://thehill.com/blogs/blog-briefing-room/news/393311-ian-bremmer-
trump-tossed-candy-to-merkel-during-g-7-said-dont
John Hodgman, interviewed by Terry Gross, "John Hodgman
Reflects on His Mother's Death and White Privilege," *Fresh Air*,
October 30, 2017
https://www.npr.org/programs/fresh-air/2017/10/30/560853843/
fresh-air-for-oct-30-2017-humorist-john-hodgman

31 **Alan Bennett**, *Keeping on Keeping on*
Peter Sagal, Paula Poundstone, and Helen Hong, on *Wait
Wait… Don't Tell Me!*, February 3, 2018
https://n.pr/2FFWq7k

32 **Trump**, *The Howard Stern Show*, April 11, 2005

33 **A. M. Rosenthal**, *Thirty-Eight Witnesses*

34 **Trump**, at a press conference after the Parkland shooting, in *NYT*
series "Guns & Gun Violence," February 22, 2018
https://nyti.ms/2sJoR2U

35 **Will Blythe,** *To Hate Like This Is to Be Happy Forever*
Trump, as quoted by Michael D'Antonio, *The Truth About Trump*
Trump, *The Apprentice,* season 8, episode 9
Trump with Schwartz, *The Art of the Deal*
Steve Nachtigall, on being Trump's childhood neighbor, in
Paul Schwartzman and Michael Miller, "Confident. Incorrigible.
Bully," *The Washington Post,* June 22, 2016
http://wapo.st/28QJIaP?tid=ss_mail&utm_term=.d63fb075de52
George W. S. Trow, *Within the Context of No Context*

37 **Trump,** quoted in Graydon Carter, "The Secret to Donald
Trump's Success," *GQ,* May 1, 1984
https://www.gq.com/story/donald-trump-gq-profile-graydon-carter
D'Antonio, "Never Enough: Donald Trump and the Pursuit of
Success," *Washington Post,* June 22, 2016
http://wapo.st/28QJIaP?tid=ss_mail&utm_term=.d63fb075de52
Robert Hass, "Bush's War," *Time and Materials*

38 **Steve Hassan,** quoted in Chauncey DeVega, "Is Donald Trump a
cult leader? Expert says he "fits the stereotypical profile," *Salon,* March 6,
2018
https://www.salon.com/2018/03/06/
is-donald-trump-a-cult-leader-expert-says-he-fits-the-stereotypical-profile/
Trump with Meredith McIver, *Trump: How to Get Rich*
Off-air conversation between Sean Hannity and Trump,
anonymous Fox News source

39 **Trump,** on his State of the Union Address, February 5, 2018
https://www.yahoo.com/news/trump-calls-dems-didnt-clap-state-union-
treasonous-un-american-210114640.html
Family friend, on Fred and Donald, in Michelle Dean, "Making
the man: to understand Trump, look at his relationship with his
dad," *The Guardian,* March 26, 2016
https://www.theguardian.com/us-news/2016/mar/26/
donald-trump-fred-trump-father-relationship-business-real-estate-art-of-deal
Trump with Schwartz, *The Art of the Deal*
https://www.bostonglobe.com/news/politics/2016/07/16/donald-trump-
ambition-and-taste-for-glitz-drove-him-surpass-his-own-father-considerable-
success/w9GNiWpAsqzbTSsgkhVBhJ/story.html
Tony Schwartz, "I Wrote 'The Art of the Deal' With Trump. His Self-
Sabotage is Rooted in his Past," *The Washington Post,* May 26, 2017
https://wapo.st/2Mm1gxN

40 **Trump**, quoted in Dean, "Making the man: to understand Trump, look at his relationship with his dad," *The Guardian*, March 26, 2016
https://www.theguardian.com/us-news/2016/mar/26/
donald-trump-fred-trump-father-relationship-business-real-estate-art-of-deal

43 **Trump**, *The Howard Stern Show*, January 7, 2004

44 **Donald Trump Jr.**, quoted in Vaughn Hillyard, "Donald Trump Jr: At Fundraiser, President's Son Says 'Zero Contact' With Dad," *NBC News*, March 12, 2017
https://www.nbcnews.com/politics/donald-trump/
donald-trump-jr-fundraiser-president-s-son-says-zero-contact-n732356
Mary Trump, to Ivanka Trump, in Caroline Mortimer, "Donald Trump's mother asked: 'What kind of son have I created?'" *The Independent*, November 4, 2017
https://ind.pn/2HIQSxT
Trump, *The Howard Stern Show*, February 27, 2006

45 **Trump**, *The Howard Stern Show*, April 11, 2005
Trump, *The Howard Stern Show*, October 10, 2006
Trump, on his daughter's beauty, *The Howard Stern Show*, January 7, 2004
Trump and Ivanka, *The View*, March 6, 2006
ttps://www.independent.co.uk/news/world/americas/us-elections/
donald-trump-ivanka-trump-creepiest-most-unsettling-comments-a-
roundup-a7353876.html
Trump, *The Howard Stern Show*, October 10, 2006
Trump, *The Howard Stern Show*, September 23, 2004
Trump and daughter Ivanka Trump, *The Wendy Williams Show*, February 28, 2013

46 **Trump**, quoted in Jamie Ducharme, "The Paralympics Fire Back After Trump Calls Them 'Tough to Watch,'" *Time*, April 28, 2018
http://time.com/5258664/trump-paralympic-games-tough-watch/

47 **Kahlil Gibran**, in Henry James Forman, "Work is Love Made Visible," *The New York Times*, July 25, 1948
https://nyti.ms/2Mpv6Bq
Trump, *The Howard Stern Show*, December 7, 2005
Trump, *The Howard Stern Show*, January 7, 2004

48 **Trump**, *The Howard Stern Show*, May 18, 2000
    Trump, *The Howard Stern Show*, December 15, 2004
    Trump, *The Howard Stern Show*, December 14, 2004

49 **Trump**, use of simile "like a dog":
    The Apprentice, season 10, episode 13,
    The Howard Stern Show, May 10, 2001
    Trump, *The Howard Stern Show*, October 10, 2001

50 **Fyodor Dostoevsky**, *The Brothers Karamazov*
    Trump, *The Howard Stern Show*, April 15, 2004
    Trump, *The Howard Stern Show*, April 11, 2005
    Charlize Theron, Jonathan Dean, "From Road Warrior to Killer
    Queen," *GQ*, May 2016
    https://www.gq-magazine.co.uk/article/
    charlize-theron-interview-british-gq-ageism-sex-appeal-south-africa

51 **Trump**, *The Howard Stern Show*, April 12, 2010
    Trump, *The Howard Stern Show*, July 15, 2008

53 **John Hawkes**, said in conversation with the author
    Trump, *The Howard Stern Show*, July 16, 2008
    Trump, *The Howard Stern Show*, October 10, 2007
    Trump, *The Apprentice*, season 6, episode 1
    Trump with Schwartz, *The Art of the Deal*

54 **Trump**, quoted in Michael Wolff, *Fire and Fury: Inside the Trump
    White House*
    Trump with Charles Leerhsen, *Trump: Surviving at the Top*
    http://www.ontheissues.org/celeb/Donald_Trump_Principles_&_Values.htm
    Trump Jr., *The Howard Stern Show*, February 27, 2006
    Trump, quoted in Wayne Barrett, *Trump: The Deals and The
    Downfall*
    Trump, *The Apprentice*, season 7, episode 5
    Trump, *The Apprentice*, season 7, episode 6

55 **Jean-Louis Comolli**, "Machines of the Visible," *Cinematic Apparatus*, eds. Teresa De Lauretis and Stephen Heath

57 **Oscar Wilde**, *The Picture of Dorian Gray*
Trump, quoted in Barrett, *Trump: The Greatest Show on Earth*
Trump, *The Howard Stern Show*, January 7, 2004
Trump, *The Howard Stern Show*, April 12, 2010
Roger Ailes, anonymous source

58 **Trump** with Schwartz, *The Art of the Deal*
Trump, *The Apprentice*, season 3, episode 5
Abe Wallach, Trump aide, *Dirty Money*, season 1, episode 6
Trump, *The Howard Stern Show*, February 6, 2013
Trump, *The Howard Stern Show*, April 16, 2004

59 **Trump**, *The Howard Stern Show*, February 6, 2013
Jake Tapper, "I Dated Monica Lewinsky," *Washington City Paper*, January 30 1998
https://www.washingtoncitypaper.com/news/
article/13014731/i-dated-monica-lewinsky
Chomsky, *Manufacturing Consent*
Trump, quoted in Corey Lewandowski, *Let Trump Be Trump*
Trump, *The Howard Stern Show*, October 10, 2007

60 **Trump**, *The Howard Stern Show*, September 22, 2005
Trump, *The Apprentice*, season 10, episode 2
Trump, as quoted by Maureen Dowd, "Introducing Donald Trump, Diplomat," *The New York Times*, August 15, 2015
https://nyti.ms/1TGI242
Jacques Lacan, *Transference: The Seminar of Jacques Lacan, Seminar VIII*

61 **Dowd**, "This is Why Uma Thurman is Angry," *The New York Times*, February 3, 2018
https://nyti.ms/2FGgHJZ

62 **Judy Berry**, "Disgusted by Men? Date Women Instead," *The Stranger*, January 31, 2018
https://www.thestranger.com/features/2018/01/31/25755863/
disgusted-by-men-date-women-instead

63 **Laurel Nakadate,** video described by Marco Bohr, "Laurel Nakadate's Controlled Voyeurism," *Visual Culture Blog,* December 3, 2011
http://visualcultureblog.com/2011/12/
laurel-nakadates-controlled-voyeurism/

64 **Paula Hawkins,** interview with *GoodReads,* December 2015
https://www.goodreads.com/interviews/show/1086.Paula_Hawkins
Ginia Bellafante, "#MeToo and the Marketing of Female Narrative," *The New York Times,* January 8, 2018
https://nyti.ms/2rqbsMj

65 **T. S. Eliot,** *Four Quartets*
Robert Stoller, "Fetish Envy," from *October,* vol. 54, The MIT Press, Autumn 1990
www.jstor.org/stable/778668
Slavoj Žižek, "From Western Marxism to Western Buddhism," *Cabinet,* Spring 2001
http://www.cabinetmagazine.org/issues/2/
Eugénie Lemoine-Luccioni, "Fetish Envy," from *October,* vol. 54, *The MIT Press,* Autumn 1990
https://www.jstor.org/stable/778668
Marjorie Garber, "Fetish Envy," from *October,* vol. 54, The MIT Press, Autumn 1990
https://www.jstor.org/stable/778668

66 **Trump,** *The Howard Stern Show,* July 16, 2008
RuPaul, "Flats are for Quitters," *Weekend Edition Sunday,* NPR, January 8, 2018
https://n.pr/2EC4Ayx
Trump with Schwartz, *The Art of the Deal*
Trump, quoted in O'Brien, *TrumpNation: The Art of Being The Donald*

67 **James McManus,** *Positively Fifth Street*
Trump, *The Howard Stern Show,* February 15, 2004
Trump, *The Howard Stern Show,* September 23, 2004

68 **André Breton,** *Nadja*
Trump, on Mike Pence, *Erin Burnett OutFront,* CNN, April 4, 2018
https://cnn.it/2IrbSpg
Trump, on beauty, *The Howard Stern Show,* January 7, 2004

Trump, *The Apprentice*, season 2, episode 11

Trump, to Hope Hicks, in Michael Woolf, *Fire and Fury*

69 **Trump**, quoted in Mark Singer, *Trump and Me*

70 **Trump and Robin Quivers**, *The Howard Stern Show*, July 16, 2008

71 **Trump**, *The Apprentice*, season 9, episode 5
Ballet adage, Emily Gordillo
Trump, *The Howard Stern Show*, April 11, 2005
Trump with Schwartz, *The Art of the Deal*
Trump with McIver, *How to Get Rich*

72 **Sean Hannity, Jessica Tarlov, and Jesse Watters**, *Hannity*,
February 1, 2018
https://youtu.be/Drr7rvM3rok
Randal Pinkett, *Dirty Money*, season 1, episode 6

73 **Trump**, *The Howard Stern Show*, February 6, 2013
Lena Dunham, tweet, November 17, 2017
https://on.mktw.net/2hBetSf
Franklin Foer, on Leon Wieseltier, "There's This Gap Between
Your Values and Lived Reality," *Slate*, November 2, 2017
http://www.slate.com/articles/double_x/doublex/2017/11/franklin_foer_
on_learning_from_the_leon_wieselter_sexual_harassment_allegations.html

76 **Trump**, to Emmanuel Macron, quoted in Ashley Parker, "'Playful
dominance': The touchy-feely relationship between Trump and
Macron," *The Washington Post*, April 24, 2018
https://wapo.st/2HpJcRL?tid=ss_tw&utm_term=.2525eeaf4ad3
Trump, at the Conservative Political Action Conference,
February 23, 2018
https://www.cnn.com/2018/02/23/politics/trump-bald-spot-hair/index.html
Trump, Stormy Daniels's discussion of Trump in *In Touch
Weekly*, May 2011
https://www.intouchweekly.com/posts/stormy-daniels-full-interview-151788
Trump, in the documentary film *You've Been Trumped*

77 **Paul Beatty**, *The Sellout*
Off-air conversation between Trump and tech, anonymous Fox
News source

78 **Kendall Jenner**, quoted in Jonathan Van Meter, "Kendall Jenner Gets Candid about Her Career, Her Controversies, and Her Private Life," *Vogue,* March 14, 2018
https://www.vogue.com/article/kendall-jenner-vogue-april-2018-issue/amp
Trump, *The Apprentice*, season 8, episode 8
Brooke Baldwin and Clay Travis, CNN, September 15, 2017
https://youtu.be/onM_uqNsoT8

80 **Arthur Schopenhauer**, *Collected Essays of Arthur Schopenhauer*
Sullivan Stapleton, Macy's Thanksgiving Day Parade, *The Today Show*, NBC, November 24, 2017
https://youtu.be/mF3voVXNFig

81 **Andy Warhol**, *Andy Warhol's Exposures*
http://www.oxfordreference.com/view/10.1093/
acref/9780191826719.001.0001/q-oro-ed4-00008309
John Updike, *Self-Consciousness*
David Foster Wallace, *This is Water*
https://fs.blog/2012/04/david-foster-wallace-this-is-water/

84 **Robert Michels**, in Robert Alan Glick, "Looking at Women: What Do Men See?" *Constructing and Deconstructing Woman's Power*
Marina Abramović, interviewed by Kate Messinger, "Marina Abramovic Thinks Sex Is Hilarious," *The Cut*, December 29, 2015
https://www.thecut.com/2015/12/marina-abramovic-feminism-sex.html

85 **Trump**, to Meat Loaf, *The Apprentice*, season 11, episode 11

86 **Peter Mountford**, "Pay Attention," *The Paris Review*, Winter 2017
https://www.theparisreview.org/fiction/7085/pay-attention-peter-mountford
Paul Solotaroff, "Trump Seriously: On the Trail With the GOP's Tough Guy," *Rolling Stone*, September 9, 2015
https://www.rollingstone.com/politics/politics-news/
trump-seriously-on-the-trail-with-the-gops-tough-guy-41447/

87 **Solotaroff**, "Kevin Durant: Why the NBA Superstar Had to Blow Up His Life to Get His Shot," *Rolling Stone*, October 19, 2016
https://www.rollingstone.com/culture/culture-sports/kevin-durant-why-the-
nba-superstar-had-to-blow-up-his-life-to-get-his-shot-114037/

88 **Bill Maher**, interview of Michael Wolff, *Real Time with Bill Maher*, January 19, 2018
https://youtu.be/M1awlyczeas

89 **Trump**, on George W. Bush, *The Howard Stern Show*, October 10, 2007

Trump, in press conference before meeting with Mueller, CNN, November 24, 2018

http://wapo.st/2DCNbIP?tid=ss_tw-bottom&utm_term=.d8b8eebb69d8

Maher, interview of Michael Wolff, *Real Time with Bill Maher*, January 19, 2018

https://youtu.be/M1aw1yczeas

Trump, *The Apprentice*, season 13, episode 11

Off-air conversation between Dana Perino and Megan McCain, anonymous Fox News source

90 **Dostoevsky**, *The Brothers Karamazov*

92 **Loudon Wainwright III**, "Motel Blues"

https://youtu.be/YfRJ87W_5Yk

THE LANGUAGE OF NEW MEDIA

95 **Mary McGrory**, in John Norris, *Mary McGrory*

96 **Drew Magary**, "Michael Wolff Did What Every Other White House Reporter Is Too Cowardly to Do," *GQ*, January 5, 2018

https://www.gq.com/story/michael-wolff-white-house-trump-access

97 **William Deresiewicz**, "In Defense of Facts," *The Atlantic*, January 2017

https://www.theatlantic.com/magazine/archive/2017/01/in-defense-of-facts/508748/

98 **Mike Holderness**, "Reality: How can we know it exists?" *New Scientist*, September 26, 2012

https://www.newscientist.com/article/mg21528841-100-reality-how-can-we-know-it-exists/

John Milton, *Apology for Smectymnuus*, section VIII

Philip Dick, *The Shifting Realities of Philip K. Dick*, ed. Lawrence Sutin

Jennifer Grossman, interviewed by Michel Martin, *All Things Considered*, NPR, "State Of The Union Speechwriter On What To Expect For Trump's Address," January 28, 2018

https://n.pr/2MfsuqG

Heraclitus, *Fragments of Heraclitus*

https://en.wikisource.org/wiki/Fragments_of_Heraclitus

99 **Noam Chomsky**, "On French Intellectual Culture and
Postmodernism," Leiden University, March 14, 2011
https://youtu.be/2cqTE_bPh7M

100 **Trump** with Schwartz, The Art of the Deal
Tom Bissell, email to the author
Trump, Ingrid Rimland, "Book Review: Wheeling with a Big
Dealer," *Los Angeles Times*, January 24, 1988
https://lat.ms/2KSYRFS
Barack Obama, Office of the Press Secretary, "Remarks by
the President at Commencement Address at Rutgers, the State
University of New Jersey," Whitehouse.gov, May 15, 2016
https://obamawhitehouse.archives.gov/the-press-office/2016/05/15/
remarks-president-commencement-address-rutgers-state-university-new

101 **E. L. Doctorow**, *The Book of Daniel*
Unnamed aide in George W. Bush Administration, quoted in
Ron Suskind, "Faith, Certainty, and the Presidency of George. W
Bush," *The New York Times*, October 17, 2004
https://nyti.ms/2Mx3SsR

102 **Stephen Marche**, "David Shields's 'Reality Hunger' in the Age
of Trump; or, How to Write Now," *Los Angeles Review of Books*,
August 5, 2017
https://lareviewofbooks.org/article/
david-shieldss-reality-hunger-age-trump-write-now/
The Michael Medved Show, author's transcription
Jeet Heer, "America's First Postmodern President," *The New
Republic*, July 8, 2017
https://newrepublic.com/article/143730/
americas-first-postmodern-president

103 **David Wojahn**, *The Writer's Chronicle*, October/November 2017
Trump, on negotiation, *The Howard Stern Show*, July 16, 2008
Trump, various typos in tweets, in Jason Silverstein and Nicole
Hensley, "The running list of typos from President Trump's
White House," *New York Daily News*, May 20, 2018
http://www.nydailynews.com/news/politics/
running-list-typos-president-trump-white-house-article-1.3186396

104 **Maher**, "Bill Maher Mocks Trump's 'Illiteracy': 'If You Can't Read,
You Can't Be President,'" *Real Time with Bill Maher*, February 9, 2018

https://www.mediaite.com/tv/
bill-maher-mocks-trumps-illiteracy-if-you-cant-read-you-cant-be-president/
Trump, on misspellings, *The Howard Stern Show*, February 6, 2013

110 **Rachel Maddow**, discussion of Roger Ailes, *The Howard Stern Show*, May 24, 2017
Margaret Atwood, *Second Words*

111 **James Parker**, "Donald Trump, Sex Pistol," *The Atlantic*, October 2016
https://www.theatlantic.com/magazine/archive/2016/10/
donald-trump-sex-pistol/497528/
Kurt Vonnegut, *Slaughterhouse-Five*
Walter Benjamin, *The Arcades Project*

112 **Jean-Francois Lyotard**, *The Postmodern Condition*
W. G. Sebald, interviewed by James Wood, *Brick*, July 10, 1997
https://brickmag.com/an-interview-with-w-g-sebald
Ronald Reagan, presidential campaign slogan, 1980
https://youtu.be/FjkX_IBYQHw
Christopher Lehmann-Haupt, review of *Trump: The Art of the Deal*, "Books of the Times," *The New York Times*, December 7, 1987
https://nyti.ms/2PbIDee
Sebastian Hied, "Existentialism and Humourism," blog, October 6, 2013
https://sebheid.wordpress.com/2013/10/06/
rashomon-and-the-postmodern-condition

113 **Michael Gove**, interviewed by Faisal Islam, *Sky News*, June 6, 2016
https://www.youtube.com/watch?v=GGgiGtJk7MA
Slavoj Žižek, on Trump, interviewed on *Channel 4 News*, February 13, 2017
https://youtu.be/ByKXcIPi7MI

114 **Peter Pomerantsev**, on the rise of the postmodern politician, *BBC Newsnight*, March 16, 2017
https://youtu.be/U5ydF5hE5Q4
David Brooks, "Vladimir Putin, the Most Influential Man in the World," *The New York Times*, April 2, 2018
https://nyti.ms/2GRYSvN

115 **Breyten Breytenbach**, "The Writer and Responsibility," *End Papers*
Jonathan Lethem, *Conversations with Jonathan Lethem*, ed.
Jaime Clarke
Trump, *CNN Money*: Interview Walk Out with Charles Feldman,
March 29, 1990
https://factba.se/transcript/
donald-trump-interview-cnn-money-march-29-1990

116 **Lev Manovich**, *The Language of New Media*
Czeslaw Milosz, described in Hass, "For Czeslaw Milosz In Krakow"
http://www.zocalopublicsquare.org/2009/08/25/
for-czeslaw-milosz-in-krakow/chronicles/poetry/

117 **Parker**, "Donald Trump, Sex Pistol," *The Atlantic*, October 2016
https://www.theatlantic.com/magazine/archive/2016/10/
donald-trump-sex-pistol/497528/
Trump, on being the Hemingway of 140 characters, "Rogue
Twitter employee deactivated Trump's personal account on last day
on the job, company says," *The Washington Post*, November 3, 2017
https://wapo.st/2MpqRG2,
Often attributed to **Hemingway**, in David Hagland, "Did Hemingway
Really Write His Famous Six-Word Story?", *Slate*, January 31, 2013
http://www.slate.com/blogs/browbeat/2013/01/31/for_sale_baby_shoes_
never_worn_hemingway_probably_did_not_write_the_famous.html

118 **Trump**, in interview with Bill O'Reilly on Putin, Fox News,
February 4, 2017
https://youtu.be/tZXsYuJIGTg
The Godfather, film
Trump, *The Howard Stern Show*, April 12, 2010

120 **Fox News source**, anonymous

121 **Andrew O'Hehir**, "The Long Goodbye," *Salon*, October 18, 2005
https://www.salon.com/2005/10/18/didion_6/
Colin Horgan, "The Reality of Donald Trump," *Medium*, October
15, 2016
https://medium.com/@cfhorgan/the-reality-of-donald-trump-633b6541198
Trump with Schwartz, *The Art of the Deal*
https://ti.me/2nCjAVj

Pam Anderson, regarding *Girl on the Loose,* E! News,
http://www.nydailynews.com/entertainment/tv-movies/
pamela-anderson-girl-loose-article-1.352967

122 **Louise Erdrich,** interviewed by David Remnick, *The New Yorker Radio Hour,* December 15, 2017
Jonathon Braun and Bill Pruitt, *Dirty Money,* season 1, episode 6

125 **Immanuel Kant,** "Idea of a Universal History on a Cosmopolitcal Plan," trans. Thomas de Quincey
https://en.wikisource.org/wiki/
Idea_of_a_Universal_History_on_a_Cosmopolitical_Plan#cite_note-1

OUT OF THE CROOKED TIMBER OF HUMANITY,
NO STRAIGHT THING WAS EVER MADE

126 **Norman Mailer,** interviewed by Martin Amis, *The Late Show,* October 23, 1991
https://youtu.be/d3eWimz4HpU
F. A. Hayek, *The Fatal Conceit*

128 **Alexis de Tocqueville,** *Democracy in America,* vol. 2
Kurt Vonnegut, *While Mortals Sleep*

129 **Jerry Brown,** *60 Minutes,* CBS, December 10, 2017
https://www.cbs.com/shows/60_minutes/
video/_EcBiZOV6lD8tNkIrNhncAgjUNf_adlv/
the-governor-who-s-castigating-the-president-on-climate-change/
Mark Turnbull, in a secretly filmed meeting with Cambridge Analytica, Channel 4 News, March 19, 2018
https://youtu.be/mpbeOCKZFfQ

130 **Dan Fleshler,** email to the author
Trump, with Gary Busey, *The Apprentice,* season 11, episode 5

131 **Associate of Trump,** quoted in Barrett, *The Greatest Show on Earth*
Richard Spencer, speech at the National Policy Institute, November 21, 2016
https://youtu.be/X2mwrrNhGdg

133 **Wilde,** *The Soul of Man Under Socialism*
Tim Parks, email to the author

134   **Louis Theroux**, interviewed by Rory Carroll, "Louis Theroux: 'For all his awfulness, I admire Trump's shamelessness,'" *The Guardian*, October 8, 2017
https://www.theguardian.com/tv-and-radio/2017/oct/08/
louis-theroux-for-all-his-awfulness-i-admire-trumps-shamelessness
Toke Dahler, on university banning controversial speakers, *BBC Newsnight*, October 29, 2015
https://youtu.be/MNRFzqQCUY8
Linda Bellos, quoted on *BBC Newsnight*, October 17, 2017
https://archive.org/details/BBCNEWS_20171017_221500_Newsnight

135   **Spencer**, speech at Alt-Right conference in Washington, DC, *National Policy Institute*, November 21, 2016
https://youtu.be/Xq-LnO2DOGE
UC Berkeley Microaggression List
https://sites.google.com/site/cacmnow/
university-of-california-microaggression-lisy

136   **Lorrie Moore**, in conversation with James Marcus, as reported to the author

138   **Brooke Gladstone**, quoted in Bradley Babendir, "The Facts Must Matter: On 'The Trouble with Reality,'" *Los Angeles Review of Books*, June 3, 2017
https://lareviewofbooks.org/article/
the-facts-must-matter-on-the-trouble-with-reality

139   **Trump**, *Larry King Live*, April 15, 1989
https://youtu.be/SCnTGhZD4ds
Trump, interviewed by Charlie Rose, 1992
https://youtu.be/2uF1K_Y692I
Wild Bill Hickok, *Deadwood*, season 1, episode 4

141   **Francine Prose**, "Finding the Fiction," *The New Yorker*, January 22, 2018
https://www.newyorker.com/magazine/2018/01/22/
letters-from-the-january-22-2018-issue
Obama, *WTF with Marc Maron*, June 22, 2016
http://www.wtfpod.com/podcast/episodes/
episode_613_-_president_barack_obama

142 **Obama**, at the White House Correspondents Dinner, April 27, 2013
https://youtu.be/ON2XWvyePH8
Obama, interviewed by Prince Harry, *BBC News*, December 27, 2017
https://youtu.be/XPGHSbJ7lxs

143 **Trump**, *Dirty Money*, season 1, episode 6
Eugene McCarthy, "The McCarthy Enigma: Minnesota Senator
Could Be Formidable If He Challenges President Johnson," *The
Washington Post*, November 12, 1967
Trump, in Barrett, *The Greatest Show on Earth*

IN PRAISE OF BLOWING SHIT UP

147 **Trump** with Schwartz, *The Art of the Deal*
Trump, *Larry King Live*, March 18, 2006
http://edition.cnn.com/TRANSCRIPTS/0603/18/lkl.01.html
Spencer, quoted in Graeme Wood, "His Kampf," *The Atlantic*,
June 2016
https://www.theatlantic.com/magazine/archive/2017/06/
his-kampf/524505/

148 **Steve Bannon**, quoted in Isobel Thompson, "Steve Bannon Says
Trump Is Fulfilling MLK's Dream," *Vanity Fair*, June 2018
https://www.vanityfair.com/news/2018/06/
steve-bannon-says-trump-is-fulfilling-martin-luther-kings-dream
K. W. Jeter, *Noir*
Josh Smith, email to the author

150 **Trump**, *The Apprentice*, season 2, episode 1
http://putlockers.la/watch/GLkleBlx-the-apprentice-season-2/episode-1.html
Joel Drucker, email to the author
Tim O'Brien, *Dirty Money*, season 1, episode 6

151 **Derek Jeter to Bush 43**, anonymous source
David Letterman, quotation of Don King, "Playboy Interview,"
Playboy, October 1984
https://playboysfw.kinja.com/
david-lettermans-1984-playboy-interview-a-candid-conv-1557838143
Lucinda Williams, quoted in Jon Michaud, "Lucinda Williams
and Painful Parts," *The New Yorker*, March 28, 2011
https://www.newyorker.com/books/double-take/
lucinda-williams-and-painful-pants

152 **James Surowiecki**, *The Wisdom of Crowds*

154 **Jimmy Breslin**, "I Run to Win," *New York Magazine*, May 5, 1969
http://nymag.com/news/politics/49901/

155 **Trump**, on toughness, *The Apprentice*, season 10, episode 4
Obama, *The Audacity of Hope*
Nicholas Montemarano, email to the author

157 **Milan Kundera**, *Life is Elsewhere*
George Orwell, *The Road to Wigan Pier*

158 **Trump**, *The Howard Stern Show*, September 2, 2005
Trump, *The Apprentice*, season 14, episode 5
Trump, Jim Moore, "Go 2 Guy: Trump card shows a bit of
ability," *Seattle Post-Intelligencer*, July 13, 2004
https://www.seattlepi.com/sports/moore/article/Go-2-Guy-Trump-card-
shows-a-bit-of-ability-1149365.php

159 **Jim Warren**, interviewed by Brian Williams, "Trump calls Russia
probe a 'hoax,'" *11th Hour with Brian Williams*, MSNBC, April 18, 2018
http://www.msnbc.com/
transcripts/11th-hour-with-brian-williams/2018-04-18
Joan Didion, "Fixed Opinions, or the Hinge of History," *The New
York Review of Books*, January 16, 2003 https://www.nybooks.com/
articles/2003/01/16/fixed-opinions-or-the-hinge-of-history/

160 **Cokie Roberts**, Josh Patashnik, "I Know Hawaii Is A State," *The
New Republic*, August 10, 2008
https://newrepublic.com/article/43442/quoti-know-hawaii-statequot

161 **Hunter Thompson**, "Fear and Loathing: The Banshee Screams
for Buffalo Meat," *Rolling Stone*, 1977
Thelonious Monk, advice to Steve Lacy, 1960
http://www.listsofnote.com/2012/02/thelonious-monks-advice.html
Barbara Kruger, "I Hate Myself and You Love Me For It,"
Esquire, May 1992
http://articles.latimes.com/1992-04-30/news/vw-1676_1_esquire-readers

162 **Richard Nash,** "What is the Business of Literature?" *VQR*, vol. 89 no. 2, March 7, 2013
https://www.vqronline.org/articles/what-business-literature
James Camp, review of Jonathan Dee's novel *The Locals*, "Bonds and Insecurities," *Bookforum,* vol. 24 no. 3, September-November 2017

163 **Tom Cotton,** Jeffrey Toobin, "Is Tom Cotton the Future of Trumpism?" *The New Yorker*, November 13, 2017
https://www.newyorker.com/magazine/2017/11/13/
is-tom-cotton-the-future-of-trumpism

166 **Michelle Obama,** Kevin Liptak, "Michelle Obama tells Ellen to 'forget what they're saying in Washington,'" *CNN Politics*, February 2, 2018
https://www.cnn.com/2018/02/01/politics/michelle-obama-ellen/index.html
Updike, *Couples*
J. M. Coetzee, *Summertime*

168 **Pablo Picasso,** quoted in Jackie Wullschlager, "Picasso's dialogue with past masters," *Financial Times*, February 27, 2009
https://www.ft.com/content/e971308e-045c-11de-845b-000077b07658

170 *One Girl's Confession*, 1953 movie poster
Simon Gray, *The Smoking Diaries*

171 **Wilde,** *The Critic as Artist*
Parker, "Donald Trump, Sex Pistol," *The Atlantic*, October 2016
https://www.theatlantic.com/magazine/archive/2016/10/
donald-trump-sex-pistol/497528/

173 **Johnny Rotten,** at the last Sex Pistols concert in San Francisco, January 14, 1978
http://ultimateclassicrock.com/the-sex-pistols-break-up/

174 **Off-air conversation between Hannity and Chris Christie,** anonymous Fox News source

175 **Noam Chomsky**, interviewed by C. J. Polychroniou, "Trump in
the White House: An Interview With Noam Chomsky," *Truthout*,
November 14, 2016
https://truthout.org/articles/
trump-in-the-white-house-an-interview-with-noam-chomsky/
Mona Chalabi, data editor for the *Guardian*, "How Can We Tell
The Good Statistics From The Bad Ones?" *TED Radio Hour*,
January 26, 2018
https://n.pr/2Ggjqes

177 **Trump**, *The Apprentice*, season 1, episode 1
Brian Williams, interview of Timothy Snyder, MSNBC,
transcribed by the author, September 16, 2017
https://archive.org/details/
MSNBCW_20170916_080000_The_11th_Hour_With_Brian_Williams

178 *The Economist*, "The deeper shifts affecting democracy in
America," *The Economist,* January 25, 2018
https://www.economist.com/books-and-arts/2018/01/25/
the-deeper-shifts-affecting-democracy-in-america
Off-air conversation between Hannity and Trump, anonymous
Fox News source

179 **Trump**, *The Howard Stern Show*, February 12, 2007
Off-air conversation between Hannity and Rand Paul,
anonymous Fox News source

180 **Trump**, quoted in Lydia O'Connor and Daniel Marans, "Trump
Condemned Racism As 'Evil.' Here Are 20 Times He Embraced
It," *HuffPost*, August 14, 2017
https://www.huffingtonpost.com/entry/
trump-racism-examples_us_5991dcabe4b09071f69b9261
Trump, asked if he'd repudiate David Duke, *Bloomberg Politics*,
August 26, 2015
https://youtu.be/gQFXYEIpdhU
Trump, speaking to the Republican Jewish Coalition, CNN,
December 3, 2015
https://youtu.be/s4_Y3YIN43c
Trump, tweet, April 24, 2013
https://twitter.com/realDonaldTrump/status/327076720425451523

181 **Trump**, quoted in Katie Little, "Donald Trump: I am the least
anti-Semitic person that 'you've ever seen in your entire life,'"
CNBC Real-Time, February 17, 2017
https://www.cnbc.com/2017/02/16/donald-trump-i-am-the-least-anti-
semitic-racist-person-that-youve-ever-seen.html
Trump, on Roy Cohn, quoted in Marie Brenner, "How Donald
Trump and Roy Cohn's Ruthless Symbiosis Changed America,"
Vanity Fair, August 2017
https://www.vanityfair.com/news/2017/06/
donald-trump-roy-cohn-relationship
Trump, tweet, June 14, 2014
https://twitter.com/realdonaldtrump/status/478018343967162369
Trump, at a rally in Youngstown, Ohio, Helena Horton, "Donald
Trump jokes about being added to Mount Rushmore—the
internet answers," *The Telegraph*, July 26, 2017
https://www.telegraph.co.uk/news/2017/07/26/
mount-trump-social-media-reacts-donald-trump-jokes-added-mount/
Trump Jr., Instagram post, 2017
https://www.instagram.com/p/BkahRHhAfa0/?utm_source=ig_embed
Trump, quoted in Jeremy Diamond, "NATO Summit: Trump
accuses Germany of being a 'captive of Russia,'" CNN Politics,
July 11, 2018
https://www.cnn.com/2018/07/11/politics/trump-germany-russia-captive-
nato/index.html

182 **Anne Carson**, *Glass, Irony and God*
Trump, *The Howard Stern Show*, February 6, 2013

184 **Mira Gonzalez** with Tao Lin, *Selected Tweets*
John Gartner, interviewed by Chauncey DeVega, "Trump's
presidency may present 'the greatest psychiatric disaster in
history,'" *Salon*, November 17, 2017
https://www.salon.com/2017/11/17/
trumps-presidency-may-present-the-greatest-psychiatric-disaster-in-history/

185 **Marie Brenner**, on the Trump family, "After the Gold Rush,"
Vanity Fair, September 1990
https://www.vanityfair.com/magazine/2015/07/
donald-ivana-trump-divorce-prenup-marie-brenner
Leslie Fiedler, in Dwight Garner, "Boom, Bust, and a Berkshires
Interloper in 'The Locals,'" *The New York Times*, August 1, 2017
https://nyti.ms/2uhPMOz

187 **Wilhelm Reich**, *The Mass Psychology of Fascism*
Jason Stanley, "Beyond Lying: Trump's Authoritarian Reality,"
The New York Times, November 4, 2016
https://nyti.ms/2ea62OH
Mussolini, quoted in Michael McDonald, "Mussolini's Jewess,"
October 11, 2014
https://www.the-american-interest.com/2014/10/11/mussolinis-jewess/

188 **Curtis**, "2014 Wipe," year-in-review short, *BBC*, December 31, 2014
https://www.realclearpolitics.com/video/2014/12/31/bbcs_adam_curtis_
on_the_contradictory_vaudeville_of_post-modern_politics.html

189 **BellKor and Netflix team**, Eliot Van BusKirk, "Bellkor's
Pragmatic Chaos Wins $1 Million Netflix Prize By Mere
Minutes," *Wired*, September 21, 2009
https://www.wired.com/2009/09/
bellkors-pragmatic-chaos-wins-1-million-netflix-prize/
Ann Coulter and Laurie Penny, *BBC Newsnight*, February 9, 2018
https://youtu.be/XV2_dw6yz2M

190 **Lesley Stahl**, at Deadline Club Awards, May 22, 2018
https://youtu.be/nq6Tt--uAfs
Johnston, *The Making of Donald Trump*
Trump with Schwartz, "Trump on Trump," *The Art of the Deal*
excerpt in *New York Magazine*, Nov. 16, 1987

191 **Adam Davidson**, *Trump: An American Dream*, documentary,
2018

192 **Pankaj Mishra**, quotation of Thomas Merton, "The Free and
the Brave," *Bookforum*, vol. 24. no. 3, September-November 2017

Trump Jr., quoted in Brennan Weiss, "Trump's oldest son said
a decade ago that a lot of the family's assets came from Russia,"
Business Insider, February 21, 2018
https://www.businessinsider.com/
donald-trump-jr-said-money-pouring-in-from-russia-2018-2

193 **Wilde**, *The Picture of Dorian Gray*
Fleshler, email to the author

194 **Former neighbor of the Trump family**, quoted in Thomas B. Edsall, "Trump Wants America to Revert to the Queens of His Childhood," *The New York Times*, April 12, 2018
https://nyti.ms/2IQupfc

195 **Trump**, on Charlottesville, Virginia, *WH.Gov*, August 15, 2017
https://youtu.be/Yyq4v005Ins
Rita Dove, "Above the Mountaintops," *The New Yorker*, November 13, 2017
https://www.newyorker.com/magazine/2017/11/13/above-the-mountaintops
Trump, reference to Elizabeth Warren at White House event, November 27, 2017
http://time.com/5038410/donald-trump-elizabeth-warren-pocahontas-2/

196 **Jacqueline Rose**, "I am a knife," *London Review of Books*, Vol. 40 No. 4, February 22, 2018
https://www.lrb.co.uk/v40/n04/jacqueline-rose/i-am-a-knife
Trump, *The Howard Stern Show*, January 7, 2004

197 **Trump**, on New York City's "Central Park Five," Miguel Marquez, *CNN* interview, 1989
https://www.cnn.com/2016/10/07/politics/trump-larry-king-central-park-five/
Trump, in response to the Orlando Shooting, June 17, 2017
http://thehill.com/blogs/blog-briefing-room/news/283991-trump-it-wouldve-been-beautiful-thing-for-fla-clubgoer-to-kill
Trump to U.S. soldiers at rally in Selma, North Carolina, November 3, 2016
http://time.com/4558173/donald-trump-military-veterans-brave-north-carolina/
Comcast Business Commercial, "Speed Always Wins," Comcast, 2016
https://www.ispot.tv/ad/AWMh/comcast-business-speed-always-wins

198 **Kundera**, *The Unbearable Lightness of Being*
Jamie Malanowski, on Barbra Streisand, "The Fine Print," *Spy Magazine*, October 1990

199 **Trump**, on race during first presidential debate, September 26, 2016
https://www.pbs.org/newshour/politics/
every-moment-donald-trumps-long-complicated-history-race
Trump, tweet, on Cinco De Mayo, May 5, 2016
https://twitter.com/realDonaldTrump/status/728297587418247168
https://www.cnn.com/2016/05/05/politics/donald-trump-taco-bowl-cinco-
de-mayo/index.html
Off-air conversation between Sean Hannity and producer,
anonymous Fox News source
Dori Monson, author's transcription of radio broadcast,
December 13, 2012

200 **Lawrence O'Donnell**, quoted in Irene Lacher, "Sunday
Conversation: Lawrence O'Donnell," *Los Angeles Times*, March
16, 2013
http://articles.latimes.com/2013/mar/16/entertainment/
la-et-st-lawrence-odonnell-msnbc-conversation-20130317
Bill Clinton, quoted in Ryan Lizza, "Let's Be Friends," *The New
Yorker*, September 10, 2012
https://www.newyorker.com/magazine/2012/09/10/lets-be-friends
Trump, in discussion with Fred Dicker, on *Talk1300*, April 14,
2017, quoted in
https://www.theatlantic.com/politics/archive/2011/04/
donald-trump-i-have-a-great-relationship-with-the-blacks/237332/

201 **V. S. Naipaul**, *A Turn in the South*
Trump, at a rally in Redding, California, *Erin Burnett OutFront*,
CNN, June 3, 2016
https://youtu.be/rOYMFkFgPzk
Sean Hannity and Ann Coulter, *Hannity*, Fox News,
November 1, 2011
https://www.huffingtonpost.com/2011/11/01/ann-coulter-herman-cain-our-
blacks_n_1069172.html
Peter Jennings, author's observation

202 **John Ridley**, discussion of Ben Carson, on *Wait Wait ... Don't Tell Me!*, 2015, author's transcription
Josh Harkinson, "Meet the White Nationalist Trying To Ride The Trump Train to Lasting Power," *Mother Jones*, October 27, 2016
https://www.motherjones.com/politics/2016/10/richard-spencer-trump-alt-right-white-nationalist
Trump, *The Howard Stern Show*, November 4, 1997

203 **Manohla Dargis**, "Glib Laughs and Race Hate," *The New York Times*, October 26, 2017
https://nyti.ms/2yN61XL
Anonymous source, off-air conversation at Fox News

APOCALYPSE ALWAYS

209 **Trump** with McIver, *How to Get Rich*
Jane Lynch, interviewed by Bill Radke on *The Record*, KUOW, November 30, 2017
http://www.kuow.org/post/record-thursday-november-30-2017
D. H. Lawrence, *The Lost Girl*
Antonio Porchia, *Voces*

212 **Michael Moore**, "5 Reasons Why Donald Trump Will Win," blog, July 23, 2016
https://michaelmoore.com/trumpwillwin/

213 **Adrian Wooldridge**, "A Conservative's Case Against Trump," *The New York Times*, January 24, 2018
https://www.nytimes.com/2018/01/24/books/review/david-frum-trumpocracy.html
Schwartz, "I Wrote 'The Art of the Deal' With Trump. His Self-Sabotage Is Rooted in his Past," *The Washington Post*, May 16, 2017
https://wapo.st/2Mm1gxN
Trump, quoted in Johnston, *The Making of Donald Trump*

214 **Glenn Kessler**, quoted in Stephanie Grace, "Just the Facts," *Brown Alumni Magazine*, January/February 2018
http://www.brownalumnimagazine.com/content/view/4506/32/
Lily Cohen, "Class Notes," *Brown Alumni Magazine*, January/February 2018

217 **Brian Williams**, quotation of Leonard Cohen, "Brian Williams is 'guided by the beauty of our weapons' in Syria strikes," *The Washington Post*, April 7, 2017
https://www.washingtonpost.com/news/morning-mix/wp/2017/04/07/beautiful-brian-williams-says-of-syria-missile-strike-proceeds-to-quote-leonard-cohen/?tid=ss_mail&utm_term=.79df91291d2f

219 **Richard Slotkin**, *Regeneration through Violence*
Joni Tevis, email exchange with the author

220 **Campbell McGrath**, interviewed by Natasha Sajé, "An Interview with Campbell," *AWP Writer*, October/November 2017
https://www.awpwriter.org/magazine_media/writers_chronicle_view/4370

221 **Nathanael West**, *The Day of the Locust*
Randy Rainbow, *The Randy Rainbow Show*, October 11, 2017
https://youtu.be/LTosB6V_V24?t=1m48s

222 **Trump**, quoted in Emily Nussbaum, "The TV That Created Trump," *The New Yorker*, July 31, 2017
https://www.newyorker.com/magazine/2017/07/31/the-tv-that-created-donald-trump

223 **Renata Adler**, *Speedboat*

224 **Trump** with Leerhsen, *Surviving at the Top*
Sigmund Freud, in Peter Gay, *Freud*
Kundera, *The Unbearable Lightness of Being*

225 **Bush 43**, in Jo Piazza and Chris Rovzar, "A Mano a Mano with Bush Duo," *New York Daily News*, November 26, 2004
http://www.nydailynews.com/archives/gossip/mano-mano-bush-duo-article-1.630291
A. C. Bradley, *Shakespearean Tragedy*

226 **Bosley Crowther**, review of *Richard III*, *The New York Times*, March 12, 1956

227 **John Hawkes**, interview in *Wisconsin Studies*, rpt. in *The Contemporary Writer 11*
Trump, in Barrett, *The Greatest Show on Earth*
Elizabeth Bowen, *The Heat of the Day*

Trump, quoted in O'Brien, "Mr. Trump Is Ready for His Close-Up. Always." *Bloomberg*, June 9, 2016
https://www.bloomberg.com/view/articles/2016-06-09/donald-trump-is-a-yuge-movie-star

228 **Harold Brodkey**, on Neal Gabler and Walter Winchell, *Sea Battles on Dry Land*
Trump, quoted in O'Brien, *TrumpNation*

229 **Roger Stone**, quoted in Carol D. Leonnig, "Mueller seeks to question Trump about Flynn and Comey departures," *The Washington Post*, January 23, 2018
http://wapo.st/2n5EOKD?tid=ss_tw&utm_term=.0ed023c519ec

230 **Trump** with Leerhsen, *The Art of Survival*

231 **Trump and Quivers**, *The Howard Stern Show*, July 16, 2008
Trump, *The Howard Stern Show*, July 16, 2008

232 **Trump**, *The Howard Stern Show*, July 16, 2008
Trump with Schwartz, on charity, *The Art of the Deal*
Kafka, *Letter to His Father*, 1966
Trump with Bohner, *The Art of the Comeback*
Trump and Quivers, *The Howard Stern Show*, October 10, 2006

233 **Trump** with Leerhsen, *Trump: The Art of Survival*
Trump, *The Howard Stern Show*, January 7, 2004
Trump, interviewed by Charlie Rose, November 6, 1992
http://vevo.site/video/RpZnPwLphOg/donald-trump-on-charlie-rose-1992.html
Trump, quoted in Marc Fisher, "The 'genius' of Trump: What the president means when he touts his smarts," *The Washington Post*, January 13, 2018
Trump, *The Apprentice*, July 2005
https://www.independent.co.uk/news/people/donald-trump-proposed-a-white-contestants-vs-black-contestants-season-of-the-apprentice-a7041971.html
Trump, on Bill Belichick, *The Howard Stern Show*, February 6, 2013
Trump, on Paris Hilton, *The Howard Stern Show*, January 7, 2004

234 **Montaigne**, *Essais*

Trump, *The Howard Stern Show*, November 9, 1999

Trump, interviewed by Charlie Rose, November 6, 1992
http://vevo.site/video/RpZnPwLphOg/donald-trump-on-charlie-rose-1992.html

Trump at Cedar Rapids rally, CNN, June 22, 2017
https://www.cnn.com/2017/06/22/politics/donald-trump-poor-person-cabinet/index.html

Trump, on *Fox and Friends*, June 25, 2017
http://video.foxnews.com/v/5482719329001/?#sp=show-clips

Trump, on his brand, *Dirty Money*, season 1, episode 6
https://youtu.be/lyuKZhsDbmM

235 **Trump**, on *Fox and Friends*, April 26, 2018
https://youtu.be/_lu_Hgw60Ns

James Comey, interviewed by George Stephanopoulos, *ABC News*, April 16, 2018
https://www.realclearpolitics.com/video/2018/04/16/comey_trump_morally_unfit_to_be_president.html

Ford Madox Ford, *The Good Soldier*

Pogo, Walt Kelly, syndicated cartoon, April 22, 1971

Deep gratitude to the following people for their invaluable research assistance: April Cavanaugh, Daniel Cecil, Kristen Coates, Emily Gordillo, Rebecca Gross, Kay Hedrick, Miran Kim, Marianne Manzler, Christian Orr, Ben Pardo, Alyson Podesta, Bernadette St. George, Sara Shapiro, Elliott Stevens, Ian Stevenson, Kristen Steenbeeke, Kimberly Swayze, and Alexander Turner.

Photo by Tom Collicott

DAVID SHIELDS is the internationally bestselling author of twenty-two books, including *Reality Hunger* (named one of the best books of 2010 by more than thirty publications), *The Thing About Life Is That One Day You'll Be Dead* (*New York Times* best-seller), *Black Planet* (finalist for the National Book Critics Circle Award), *and Other People: Takes & Mistakes* (*NYTBR* Editors' Choice). The film adaptation *of I Think You're Totally Wrong: A Quarrel* was released by First Pond Entertainment in 2017. *The Trouble With Men: Reflections on Sex, Love, Marriage, Porn, and Power* is forthcoming in 2019. A recipient of Guggenheim and NEA fellowships and a senior contributing editor of *Conjunctions,* Shields has published essays and stories in the *New York Times Magazine, Harper's, Esquire, Yale Review, Salon, Slate, McSweeney's,* and *Believer.* His work has been translated into two dozen languages.

dshields@davidshields.com
davidshields.com
instagram.com/_davidshields
facebook.com/davidshieldswriter
twitter.com/_DavidShields

THOUGHT
CATALOG
Books

Thought Catalog Books is a publishing house owned by The Thought & Expression Company, an independent media group founded in 2010 and based in Brooklyn, NY. Committed to facilitating thought and expression in order to engender a more attentive, imaginative, and exciting world, we aim to help people become better listeners and communicators.

Powered by Collective World, we're a community of creative people across the globe. Visit us on the web at thoughtcatalog.com or explore more of our books at shopcatalog.com. If you'd like to join our community, apply at www.collective.world.

CPSIA information can be obtained
at www.ICGtesting.com
Printed in the USA
LVHW030102171218
600706LV00001B/152/P